NUMBER 575

THE ENGLISH EXPERIENCE

ITS RECORD IN EARLY PRINTED BOOKS
PUBLISHED IN FACSIMILE

JEAN CALVIN

APHORISMES
OF CHRISTIAN RELIGION

LONDON, 1596

DA CAPO PRESS
THEATRVM ORBIS TERRARVM LTD.
AMSTERDAM 1973 NEW YORK

The publishers acknowledge their gratitude to
the Syndics of Cambridge University Library
for their permission to reproduce the
Library's copy, Shelfmark: Syn.8.59.56

S.T.C.No. 4374

Collation: $*^4$, A-N^8, O^4

Published in 1973 by

Theatrum Orbis Terrarum Ltd.,
O.Z. Voorburgwal 85, Amsterdam

&

Da Capo Press Inc.
- a subsidiary of Plenum Publishing Corporation -
277 West 17th Street, New York N.Y. 1011
Printed in the Netherlands
ISBN 90 221 0575 x
Library of Congress Catalog Card Number:
73-6107

1774821

APHORISMES OF
CHRISTIAN RE-
LIGION:
OR,

A VERIE COMPENDIOVS
abridgement of M. I. Calvins Institutions, set forth in short sentences me-
thodically by M. I. Piscator:

And now Englished according to the Authors
third and last edition,
By H. Holland.

Be not caried about with diuerse and strange doctrines:
for it is a good thing that the heart be esta-
blished with grace, &c. Heb.13.9.

AT LONDON,
Imprinted by Richard Field and Robert Dexter,
and are to be sold in Paules Churchyard, at
the signe of the Brasen serpent.
1596.

TO THE REVE-
REND FATHER, THE
RIGHT WORSHIPFVLL
Mr. D Goodman, Deane of Weſt-
minſter, grace and peace by
Ieſus Chriſt.

E ſee (right wor-
ſhipfull) that a
great nūber (bleſ-
ſed bee God for
our happy peace,
and this ſweete
calme ſo long continued) haue attained ſome knowledge of God by
the preaching of the Goſpell: yet
but few I feare, haue truly learned
and knowen Chriſt : for the wordes Ephe.4.19.
20.
of Iohn are, *He that ſinneth, hath neither* 1.Iohn.3.6.

* iij

ſeene nor knowne him. And Gregorie

Gregor. Pa-
ſtoral. cur. 1.
pars.cap.2.
ſaith truly; *Viuendo conculcant, quæ non
opere ſed meditatione didicerunt.* Looke
what knowledge is attained by bare
ſpeculation, without experience of
faith, and practiſe of life, it is but a
dimme light ſoone quēched. Light
is good, & the firſt ſtep to life, dark-
neſſe is euill and daungerous, and
the way that leadeth vnto death, &

Iohn.3.19.
yet moſt men *loue darkeneſſe more then
light, becauſe their deeds are euill.* VVher-
fore to helpe forwards this kinde of
men, which do but ſip and taſt but
litle of holy religion, I haue ſpent
ſome houres to tranſlate this little
treatiſe, which will giue the willing
mind in a very ſmall time a ſynopſis
or ſhort view of the whole bodie of

Three times
publiſhed in
Latin.
Gods holy truth, the pure worſhip
and ſeruice of God. It hath done
much

much good, no doubt in Latin, and
I truſt it ſhall by Gods bleſſing and
goodneſſe, profite ſome in Engliſh.

The ſame reaſons which moued
the author to commend this booke
to that good, old, & reuerēd father
M. Beza (his age, his place and calling, his ſpeciall loue and affection
towards him) were motiues alſo vnto me (right worſhipfull) to recom-
mend the ſame vnto you: for your
Chriſtian care, & fatherly loue and
affection towardes me, I find to be
ſuch, not in words but in deeds, that
I may and muſt nothing doubt of
your fauorable acceptation. Next
for the gift (the booke I meane) it is
the ſame: for the outward coate and
colours are onely changed, but the
ſubſtaunce and matter is the ſame.
And as for my loue towardes you, I

* iiij

can no way teſtifie it as I would, but
vnto God onely in prayer for you:
The Lord God cōtinue your good
health , and graunt you the good
comfortes of his holie ſpirite , the
peace which paſſeth all vnderſtanding in this life, and an euerlaſting
reſt in the kingdome of glorie, by
and through Ieſus Chriſt our alone
Sauiour and redeemer. Amen. The
yeare of Chriſt. 1596. Maij. 18.

Your worſhips euer to vſe
in the Lord Chriſt.

Henr. Holland.

To the Reader.

Hou haſt here (Chriſtian Reader) an abridgement or short vew of *Mr. Caluins Inſtitutions*, a worke ſo much commended for many yeares, and ſo embraced and publiſhed in all reformed Churches & in all languages Latin, French, Dutch, English &c. as no one worke of any late writer hath had the like acceptation and generall approbation. The learned profeſſors and readers in open ſcholes haue yearely read ouer, and commended this worke vnto their auditories, as the Schoole men in the blind age haue done the *Mr. of Sentences*, and others of late yeares *Phil. Melanɭth Common Places*. It was not the authors meaning, nor my deſire to make any man negligent, in peruſing the great worke it ſelfe, but rather to

Maſter Caluins Inſtitutions read in opē ſcholes, as Pet. Lumbard, by the Schoolemē. Philip. Mel. by Pezellius.

A

excite and helpe flow wits to search into the fountaine, whence these small braunches are deriued. Let this little booke be therfore vnto thee, but as a methodicall index, to helpe and confirme memorie.

The world is full of bookes, but few good: The light is great, I wish it may be greater, for light is good and darknes euill. It is granted of all men that the essentiall difference betweene man and beast is reason, the light of nature; but betweene man and man the speciall difference is Religion: betweene true Religion and the false, the light of God, Gods holy written truth. The Turkish Paganisme hath an Alcoron: the Papacie is grounded vpō the traditiōs of mē, the naturall man the seruant of sin will hearken, beleeue and follow the poore light of blind reason, blind sense, Iam.1.13.14. *and what is more daungerous, his most blind and corrupt concupiscence the mother of all sin: So let the seruant of Christ, harkē, beleeue & obey the holy Gospell of Iesus Christ. If mē will not heare, they cā not learne: if they will* Rom.10.14. *not learne, they cā not know, if they will not know, they can not beleeue: if they do not beleeue, they cā not loue: if they do not loue, they*

can

can not truſt : if they do not truſt , they haue
no ſounde feare : if there be no ſounde feare,
they be not humbled : if they be not humbled,
they can not worſhip God : if they be not true
worſhippers, they can not be ſaued.

Concerning my tranſlation , I haue not
followed the authours vvordes , but I truſt I
haue his meaning in plaine and beſt knowen
termes . I remenber the vvitty Poet which
taught in me youth:

> Non verbum verbo curabis reddere fidus
> Interpres———

Horat. arte
Poetic.

Againe, for my boldneſſe & libertie ſom-
times in omiſſion, ſometimes in addition of
vvordes and ſome few ſentences : I haue the
authour himſelfe for example, as may appeare
in the Epiſtle following . There is nothing
materiall pretermitted. I amplified no where
ſo much as in the doctrine of the Lordes Sup-
per(and there not much) for the better vn-
derſtanding of ignoraunt people , vvhich ſo
much in moſt places prophane the ſame.

I know that Gregory ſaith right vvell &
truly, ars artium eſt regimen animarū, *the*
gouernement & care of ſoules is the beſt arte
& facultie on earth: & again, Præconis of-

Gregor. Pa-
ſtor. cur. 1. p.

To the Reader.

2.Cor.2.16.

ficium fufcipit quifquis ad facerdotiũ ac-
cedit, vt ante aduentum iudicis, qui terri-
biliter fequitur , ipfe fcilicet clamando
gradiatur: *that euerie Minifter of Chrift*
as a crier muft go on before, and that the
dreadfull iudge of all the vvorld followes af-
ter : who then is fufficient for thefe things?
True it is, that the preaching of the Gofpell
muft be our greateft care. I fpēd therfore but
fome houres for my refreshing, as it vvere
on this manner . I truft to offend none iuft-
ly, my hope is to do good to fome, and my de-
fire is to many . The Lord Chrift fchoole vs,
and prepare vs for his kingdome.

Thine in Chrift Iefu,
Henry Holland.

Thi

THis copie paſt from my ragged hand after the firſt writing to the preſſe immediatly : for the whole worke had not aboue ſix whole dayes. The worke-men were wearied with the hand, and the haſt might haue cauſed many errours.Wherfore I muſt deſire thee, good Reader, friendly to correct theſe few faults which haue eſcaped.

Errata.

Pag.1.marginall note or, for, as. pag.1.Aphoriſ. 3.of yeares and iudgement. pag.22.Aphoriſ.3. commendeth for commandeth. pag.39.Aphoriſ.2 ſupply as if they had read. pag.42. Aphoriſ.11. put out ſitting. pag.48. Aphoriſ.17. which came of, for which came not of Abrah. pag.56. firſt line, the laſt, for and at the laſt. pag.69. Aphoriſ.9. reade by faith imputed vnto vs. pag.115. Aphoriſ 5.7.8. in for into.pag.125. Aphoriſ.6.of for and. pag.144. Aphoriſ.16. were for we. pag.172.ſe& 8. panem Domini and panem Dominum tranſpoſed. pag.181.Aphor.14.put out that.

THE AVTHORS PRE-
face to Maiſter Beza.

 Suppoſe you can re-
member(right reue-
rend) what moued
our friend *Caſpar O-
leuian*, a man of bleſ-
ſed memorie to pub-
liſh his abridgement
of that great worke,
of that right worthie man of God Maiſter
Caluin , I meane his Inſtitutions : to wit,
partly to helpe the Miniſters of the Goſpell through Germanie to teach Chriſt
ſoundly : for he thought the prolixitie of
that volume debarred a great number frõ
reading it : partly alſo and principallie for
the benefit of our ſchoole he gaue a ſum-
marie expoſition thereof, handling euery three monethes or quarter , one booke

or

or part of the whole, so that he finished & perfected yearely the Summe of Christian Religio. And I trust the Lord gaue a blessing vnto that his worke, & that many haue profited thereby, which vouchsafed the reading of the same, & as for my scholers, which haue heard his readings, I am wel assured they haue profited much therby. But whenas he was take by death from vs in the midst of his labours and translated to the celestiall schoole ; the necessitie of this place so requiring & dutie binding me, & as the brethre (which the were to prouide for this schoole) desired: I did succeed Oleuian in this worke : & so anon after his death I began to expounde the abridgement of Caluins Institution vnto mine auditorie , and in one halfe yeare space (for sooner I could not well do it) I finished the same.

And when my Scholers desired for their furtherace in Diuinitie, that I would take the paines to appoint the some Logicall disputations: I soone granted their requeft: and therfore to proceede in some lawfull and good courfe , for their more

Oleuians Epitome.

A iiij

ſpeedie and better profite I did reduce e-
uery point of Chriſtian doctrine, ſo ſoone
as I finiſhed any place in the Inſtitution,
into ſome few Aphoriſmes, and the ſame
I propounded vnto them for diſputation.
And this was the firſt cauſe of writing
theſe Aphoriſmes: In collecting them I
haue vſed Chriſtian libertie, I haue not
followed the very wordes of the authour
(for that could not well be done, the authors ſtile being full and large, and Aphoriſmes requiring breuitie) and I added
ſome thing in the ſentences, which is not
in that abridgment: yet the worke agreeth
wel, as I thinke, and as the brethren iudge,
with the authors doctrine, and ſpecially
with the holy Scriptures.

    Again, I rather call theſe ſentences, A-
Theſes. phoriſmes, then (as they be called vſually)
theames, or queſtions, for the word *theſis*
carieth ſome ſigne of doubtfulneſſe with
it, as may be ſeene with Ariſtotle in his
Topickes, where diſputers are ſaid *aliquid*
τιθέναι to ſet downe ſome thing, which
they do not auouch to be true: for the Lo-
gitian, ſaith Ariſtotle in thoſe bookes,
                        muſt

must not affirme any thing as truth, but
this belongeth to him onely which can
bring proofe by demonstratiue conclusi-
ons: but such as dispute Logically, are
ready to defend their position as true, or
at least wise as probable. And some time
the word *thesis* with Aristotle signifieth
some absurde opinion: caried about vnder the name of some famous Philoso-
pher. But these sentences contained in
these Aphorismes are neither absurde
(but to such wits as be not inlightned and
sanctified by Gods spirite) nor such as any
Christian may lawfully doubt off. Here
some man will aske; wherefore then are
they propounded to be disputed vpon,
and so to be called in question? I answer,
albeit we dispute of them, yet we doubt
not of the truth of them: for that is not the
end wherefore we propose them in dispu-
tation: but that our auditorie may the better see and know the truth of them, and to
be more assured of the same, by hearing
all obiections of heretickes, and all scru-
ples that may sticke in their mindes an-
swered and resolued by the word of God:

and fo both the ignorant receiue better inftruction, and the weaker confirmation in the heauenly truth . But fome will fay; what neede was there thefe Aphorifmes fhuld be publifhed, feeing they were written for the fpecial and proper vfe of thine auditorie? I haue herein alfo followed M. Oleuian that moft faithfull Minifter and feruaunt of Chrift: for his defire was that his abridgments might not only benefite fuch as heard him here, but ftraungers alfo of other countreys . If he thought his abridgement fhould pleafe many becaufe of breuitie , much more may I expect the like fauour, for that I am herein more compendious then he . For thefe fhort Aphorifmes containe the chiefe points of Chriftiã Religion barely propounded, much like a withered body , or certaine iointes and bones without skinne, flefh or fynewes, fuch as Anatomiftes referue for demonftration fake . So here we haue taken away the fulnes and glory of that ftile, as the skinne and flefh therof: but the fentences, which appertaine to any one place of Chriftian doctrine, (as things which

moft

σκελετόν,

moſt conceme the perfection of a body)
are like bare and naked bones knit and
iointed one with an other. But ſome will
ſay, that this is but dry and bare ſtuffe in
deede, without any ſap or grace in it. I anſwer and graunt theſe bones be but bare,
yet are they bones, that is, firme and ſolid
things indeede, which neither want good
ſynewes, nor iuice and marow of heauenly doctrine in them. Such as deſire a more
copious ſtile, let them either reade that a-
bridgement, or the authours great worke
it ſelfe. For my drift was not in this labour, to withdraw any man from the authours worke: but rather to giue an eaſie
introduction therunto, and to winne, and
to excite ſuch as fauour holy Religion, the
more to embrace tha tworke. For I truſt,
that he which vnderſtandeth the chiefe
grounds of Gods truth, ſet forth and contained in theſe Aphoriſmes (if he be caried with a true zeale to learne and receiue the knowledge of Gods heauenly
veritie) ſhall the rather deſire to ſee theſe
points in the author himſelfe, where they
are more fully diſputed and handled.

Now it remaineth moſt worthy and reuerend Beza, that I ſhew what moued me
to commende and dedicate theſe Aphoriſmes vnto you. Firſt this haue I done to
gaine this little worke the more grace &
fauour among men , as being approued
by a man which hath , and yet doth beſt
merite of the Church of our age & time.
And herin alſo I thought it beſt to follow
M. Oleuian, who in like manner ſought
protection and grace for his worke vnder
your name. Wherefore hauing thus both
one drift and ſcope , to inſtruct ſoundly
(ſuch youth as deſire the knowledge of
holy Scriptures ,) in the principles of
Chriſtiā Religion, as ſhortly as may be, it
was my deſire alſo to ſend vnto you , & ſo
to cōmende vnto the Church of God this
little worke , vnder your moſt worthie
name ſo much commended (as Oleuian
ſpeaketh) and ſo much accounted among
all the faithfull.

Next , my good will was to giue ſome
publique teſtimony of my dutifulneſſe towardes you, and ſo to confirme my Scholers by my example, in that reuerend opinion

nion which they haue already conceiued
of your felfe, and of your writings, and to
whet their loue & zeale to know the fame.
For albeit your name be long fince verie
pretious & great, and for good caufe, with
them which fauour the truth in moft fyn-
ceritie, fo as here my commendation is
needleffe: yet this I truft fhal ad fome confirmatiō of that reuerend opinion which
thefe haue conceiued of you.

   And laftly I defired alfo hereby to re-
quite your loue teftified towardes me by
fo many approued teftimonies as you
haue written louing letters vnto me : for
that reuerend mention of me in your laft
writings, but fpecially in your moft paine-
ful and learned annotations vpon the new
Teftament: for albeit I thinke not my felfe
therefore happy, for that any mortall man
thinks fo reuerently of me, commending
my poore labors to the Church of Chrift:
for I haue learned of the Apoftle, that
prayfe to be founde and true, which fhalbe giuen of God to euery man in the laft
day : yet it can not be but comfortable to
any good man, to haue the commenda-

tion, of any one who is well knowen and moſt highly and worthily commended for wiſedome and pietie. Now I pray the Lord God, and Father of our Ieſus Chriſt bleſſe our labours and godly deſires : that all ſtudents in the Scriptures, may by ſuch helpes dayly profite in the knowledge of the heauenly truth : that whatſoeuer they haue well and rightly learned, they may alſo profitably and ſoundly teach the peo-ple of God, to the glory of Gods name and their owne euerlaſting ſal-uation in Chriſt Ieſu.
Amen.

A

A Table of the common places
handled in this booke.

Of

CHAP. 1.

Of the knowledge of God.

✳ I. APHORISME.

 E know God either as ᵃ creator, or as ᵇ redeemer.

II.

The knowledge of God as
he is creator, is double: The one naturall,
the other attained.

III.

The naturall knowledge of God as he
is creator, is that which naturally appeareth in such as be of yeares of iudgement,
for such ᶜ without instructiõ are perswaded
that God is, or some diuine essence, eternall, most mightie, most wise, most blessed: maker and gouernour of the world, &
of all things therein: & therefore that this
God must be religiously worshipped.

IIII.

That such knowledge of God is natu-

*An Apho-
risme is a short
sentence sele-
cted and set a-
part, or a defi-
nition, distin-
ction,&c.*

a Act.14.15
16 17.and
chap.17.24.
25,&c.
Rom.1.19. 20
b Iohn.17.3.

c Rom.1.18.
19 & chap.2
14.15.

B

rally ingraffed in the mindes of men, may appeare, partly for that barbarous natiōs exercife fome religious ceremonies: partly alfo for that the prophane contemners of God are otherwhiles fmitten with a moft great feare when God fheweth fome fignes of his maieftie:as in thunders and lightnings.

V.

The knowledge of God as he is creator is attained, both by humane or Philofophicall fpeculation and confideration of the ᵃ workes of God : and by diuine inftruction, ᵇ by the very written word of God.

ᵃ Rom.1.20
ᵇ Gen.1.
Iob.38.39.40
41.
Pfal.19.104.
Prou.8.22.
&c.

VI.

The naturall knowledge of God, and that alfo which is attained by mans induftrie,yeeld fome feede of Religion:but the fame is fo corrupted partly by ignorance, partly by malice, that of it felf it can breed in vs but onely ᶜ fuperftition and falfe Religion.

ᶜ Rom.1.21.
21.23.
Act.17.22.
&c.
1.Cor.12.2.

VII.

And for the knowledge of God as he is creator,attained by the word of God, the
fame

fame is either naked and bare, or ioyned
with fome affection of pietie.

VIII.

This laft degree of knowledge excelleth all the reft: yet it fufficeth not for the
true worfhip of God, and mans true felicitie, but is fufficient onely (as the former
degrees) to make a man[a] inexcufable. We
muft haue alfo by the[b] word, the knowledge of God as redeemer, and the fame
linked & knit with the faith and affurance
of Gods children. And this is that which
is worthily called a true[c] & a fauing knowledge of God, whereby God as he is both
creatour and redeemer is acknowledged
and rightly worfhipped: and whereby alfo
we become bleffed.

[a] *Rom.1.20.*

[b] *Pfal.19. by confer.v.8.& the v. folow-ing with the precedent.*

[c] *Iohn,17.3*

CHAP. II.

Of the holy Scripture.

I. Aphorisme.

THe holy Scripture is that which holy
[a]men fpecially the[b]Prophets and[c] A-
poftles,[d]moued by the infpiration of the
holy Ghoft, haue written to[e] teach the

[a] *2.Tim.3.16.*
1.Pet.1.21.
[b] *Ibid.*
[c] *Rom.1.2.*
2.Pet.1.19.
[d] *2.Pet.3.15.16.*
[e] *Rom.15 4.*
1.Tim.4.19.16.
2.Tim.3.15.16.17.
Iohn.5 39. & Chap.20.31.

people of God the pure worſhip of God,
and what is mans true happineſſe . Sometimes it is called Gods written word , and
the ſacred Scriptures: & ſometimes without an epithet, the Scriptures , and in the
ſingular number,the Scripture:ſomtimes
in Latin *Biblia,* of the Greeke word in the
plurall number βιβλία, bookes : but this
name other nations alſo vſe in the ſingular number,*Bible.*

II.

The holy Scripture is diuided into the
bookes of the old and of the new Teſtament , or couenaunt: for that it was written partly before , partly after the incarnation of Chriſt: The firſt part is called,
bookes or writings Propheticall , the ſecond Apoſtolicall.

III.

In the old Teſtament are numbred 24.
bookes:yet ſo as we count the ſtorie of Sa-
muell, of the Kings , and of the Chronicles , and the 12 . ſmall Prophets ,to haue
but one ſeuerall booke in euerie ſtory:as
may appeare in this table folowing.

1. Geneſis

1. Genesis, or the 1.booke of Moses.
2. Exodus, or the 2.booke of Moses.
3. Leuiticus, or the 3.booke of Moses.
4. Numeri, or the 4.booke of Moses.
5. Deuteron.or the 5.booke of Moses.
6. Iosua.
7. Iudges.
8. Ruth.
9. Samuels 2.bookes, commonly called 1.and 2.of Kings.
10. Kings 2.bookes, called also 3.and 4. of Kings.
11. Chronicles 2.bookes.
12. Ezra.
13. Nehemia.
14. Hester.
15. Iob.
16. The booke of Psalmes.
17. The Prouerbes of Salomon.
18. Ecclesiastes or the Preacher.
19. Canticles, or Song of Salomon.
20. Esayah.
21. Ieremy:ad here his Lamentations.
22. Ezechiell.
23. Daniell.

24. The
ſmall Pro-
phets. 12.

1. Hoſea.
2. Ioel.
3. Amos.
4. Obadaiah.
5. Ionas.
6. Michah.
7. Nahum.
8. Habacuc.
9. Zephaniah.
10. Haggai.
11. Zachariah.
12. Malachi.

The bookes of the new Teſtament
are 27. which are theſe:

1. The Goſpel according to S.Mathew.
2. The Goſpell according to S.Marke.
3. The Goſpell according to S.Luke.
4. The Goſpell according to S.Iohn.
5. The Actes of the Apoſtles.
6. Pauls Epiſtle to the Romaines.
7. Epiſtle 1. to the Corinthians.
8. Epiſtle 2. to the Corinthians.
9. Epiſtle to the Galathians.
10. Epiſtle to the Epheſians.
11. Epiſtle to the Philippians.

12. Epiſtle to the Coloſſians.
13. 1.Epiſtle to the Theſſalonians.
14. 2.Epiſtle to the Theſſalonians.
15. 1.Epiſtle to Timothie.
16. 2.Epiſtle to Timothie.
17. Epiſtle to Titus.
18. Epiſtle to Philemon.
19. Epiſtle to the Hebrues.
20. The Epiſtle of S.Iames.
21. 1.Epiſtle of S.Peter.
22. 2.Epiſtle of S.Peter.
23. 1.Epiſtle of S.Iohn.
24. 2.Epiſtle of S.Iohn.
25. 3.Epiſtle of S.Iohn.
26. Epiſtle of Iude.
27. The Reuelation of S.Iohn.

IIII.

This Scripture, or the word of God contained in this Scripture, is the ªrule both of faith and life, for all the true worſhippers of God: becauſe God is the ᵇ author of it, who cannot lye, and hath authoritie to commaunde all men: and therefore auncient writers call them, bookes canonicall, or Canonicall Scriptures. Vnto this volume alſo are vſually

a 2.Pet.1.19

b 2.Tim.3. 16.
2.Pet.1.21.

nnexed certaine other bookes which are
alled Apocrypha,that is,bookes kept hid
: secret: for that we must not bring these
) light when we are to confirme any doctrine concerning faith or Gods worship
by diuine testimonies.

V.

And as for the absolute authoritie of
this Scripture , it consisteth in those very
words wherein it was first written,for that

a 2.Tim.3.
1*6*.
2.Pet.1.21.

the same words were spoken ª by the holy
Ghost vnto these holy writers : and they
are Hebrue in the old , and Greeke in the
new Testament.The translations or inter-
pretations of other languages haue their
credit and authoritie , as they be founde
to agree with the first fountaines whence
they are deriued.

V I.

And albeit this Scripture ought to be
receiued of all mē , for that it came by the

a Es.59.21.
Iohn.14 26.
and 15.26.&
16.13.
Rom 8.16.
1.Ioh.2 27.
& chap.5.6.

inspiration of Gods spirit, and is of credit
sufficient of it selfe : yet before the same be
sealed in our harts by the ª holy Ghost, we
cannot haue any certain knowledge of the
power thereof;that so we may with full af-
surance

furance truſt thereunto.

VII.

And yet we finde certaine proofes (as mans reaſon can conceiue) good for the confirmation of the Scripture vnto vs, as theſe folowing; the maieſty of that heauēly doctrine, the ſimplicitie, puritie and excellencie of the ſtile: the conſent alſo of all partes, the admiration whereunto it carieth vs, the antiquitie of the bookes, ſo many and ſo wonderfull miracles, the admirable complement of all Prophecies, the diuine preſeruation of theſe bookes againſt the furie of the enemies, the conſent of the Church, the bloud of Martyrs, and laſtly the common ſtate and conditiō of thoſe men which firſt writte the ſame.

VIII.

And albeit the cōſent of the Church be a great argumēt to commende the authoritie of the Scripture vnto vs, yet the Popiſh aſſertiō is falſe, that the authoritie of the Scripture doth hāg vpō the iudgmēt of the Church: as if we could not beleeue the Scripture, or as if the Scripture were not to be truſted, if the iudgement of the

Church did not moue vs thereunto, by teſtifying that theſe are the holy Scriptures,
and commaunding vs to reuerence them
as the truth.

IX.

Neither yet doe we here deſpiſe the
iudgment of the Church, whē we aſcribe
not therunto that which is due vnto God,
which is to aſſure vs of the truth of this celeſtiall doctrine. We muſt I graunt highly eſteeme of the teſtimonie of the true
Church. For the Church (as a Notary)
keepeth the holy Scriptures: and diſcer-
neth the true Scriptures of God from the
falſe : as the goldfiner trieth and diſcer-
neth gold frō copper by his touch-ſtone,
and as a skilfull man can teach vs to know
good coyne, which the ignorant knoweth
not. Againe, the true Church(as a cōmon
cryer) doth publiſh the Scriptures: and
laſtly doth rightly interpret the ſame.

X.

Foraſmuch as the onely Hebrue text
in the old Teſtament, and the Greeke in
the new is authēticall, & hath abſolute authoritie: the Councel of Trent conſequēt-

ly

ly muſt erre, where it giueth caution, to hold the Latin old vulgar edition as authenticall, in all publique readings, diſputations, ſermons and expoſitions: and that no man be ſo bold or preſume to reiect it vnder any colour.

XI.

And ſeeing the Scripture is giuen to inſtruct vs, concerning Gods worſhip & our ſaluatiõ, thoſe phantaſticall wits muſt erre, which laying aſide the Scripture flye vnto reuelations.

XII.

And whereas the ſcope of God in the Scripture, is to teach men concerning his holy worſhip and mans true happineſſe; it foloweth then that it is ſo abſolute & perfect, that it containeth all things needfull for this end & purpoſe. For otherwiſe we ſhould ſay that God himſelfe doth not attaine that which he purpoſed, and this to ſpeake, is againſt the omnipotécy of God.

XIII.

If the doctrine of the ſcripture be ᵃ perfect, comprizing all points which neceſſarily concerne Gods pure worſhip & our

ᵃ 1.Tim, 3. 16.17.& Pſa. 19.7.8.9.

saluation:then it foloweth that the Papists erre, which thrust vpon vs their vnwritten verities; traditions, I say, which neither Prophets nor Apostles haue euer writtē.

XIIII.

And for that the doctrine of the Scripture is vndoubtedly [a] true:for that it came by the [b] inspiration of the holy Ghost: that must of necessitie be erroneous which is contrary vnto it: as some fewe traditions are, which the Papistes thrust vpon the Church, as the very word of God it selfe.

a 2.Pet.1.19
b Ibid.21. 2.Tim.3.16.

CHAP. III.

Of God.

I. Aphorisme.

GOd is a [a] spirite, most [b] pure, [c] infinite, [d] eternall, [e] immutable: [f] almighty, most [g] wise, [h] good, [i] louing, [k] mercifull, [l] iust, [m] holy, [n] true & of most free [o] & absolute authoritie: and is [p] Father, Sonne & holy spirite: creator of heauen and [q] earth & of all things which are contained in them: the [r] redeemer and [s] sanctifier of al[l h]is elect.

a Iohn.4.24.
b Deut.6.4. Exo.3.14.15.
c Psal.139.7 &c. Es.66.1. Ier.23.23 24 1.Kings.8.27.
d Rom.1.20 and 23. 1.Tim.1.17. Psal.102.25.&c.Reu.1.8.
e Psal.102 27.28, Mal.3.6.Es.4[...] 10.Rom.11.

29. *f* Gen.17.1.and c.35.11.Exod.15.Iob 38.39.Psal.91.1.2. *g* Psal. 139 1.104.24.147.5. 1.Sam.16 8. Heb.4.13.Rom.11.33.34.and 16.27. 1.Tim 1.17. *h i k l* Exod.34.6.and 7. *h* Psal.5.13.and 34.9 51.20. & 52.last v.54 8.9. *i k* Ion.4.2. *l* Gene.18.23.25.Deut.32.4.Iob. 34.10. 11.12 & 36.chap.Psal.11.last v.34 16.17.Prou 8.8.Es.45.11.Ierem.12.1. Lam.1.8. *m* Leu.19.2.Iosh 24.19.1.Sam.2.2.Psal.99 3.Es.6 3. *n* Psa. 36.6 Heb.6.17.18.Tit.1.2. *o* Rom.9 15,&c. Math.20.15. *p* Math.28. 19. *q* Gen.1.1. *r* Luk.1.68,&c. *s* Ephe.2.10.

II.

These three the Father, Sonne, & holy Ghost are three distinct[a] persons:and euery person very[b] God : yet not three Gods, but they are that[c] one very God, which in the Scripture is called *Iehouah* the Lord.

[a] Heb.1.3.
[b] Iohn.1.1. Act.5 3.&4.
[c] Deut.6.4.

III.

These three persons differ, & are distinguished, for that the Father is ofnone: the Sonne is of the[a] Father by an incomprehensible and inspeakable[b] generation: The holy Ghost is of the[c] Father & of the[d] Sonne by an incomprehensible and inspeakable[e] proceeding.

[a] Iohn.1.14
[b] Psal.2.7. Prou.8.24. and 25.
[c] Iohn.15.26
[d] Ibid. Rom.8.9.
[e] Iohn.15.26 1 Iohn.5.7.

CHAP. IIII.

Of the Angels.

I. Aphorisme.

THe Angels are[a] spirituall[b] creatures, which[c] minister vnto God the creator.

[a] Psal.104.4.
[b] &Heb.1.7. &last Eph.6. 12. Heb.1.7. Coloss.1.16.
[c] Heb.1.v.last 1.K.22.20.&c

II.

Of the Angels, fome are good, fome are euill.

III.

The good Angels are they which haue ftoode and continued in their perfection, wherein they were created, and haue receiued their [a] confirmatiō: & therfore are euer ready [b] to glorifie God in all obedience: for which caufe they did appeare in certaine winged pictures (which are called [c] Cherubins and [d] Seraphins) formed like men to the people [e] of Ifraell, and to the Prophets [f] Efay & [g] Ezechiell, to fignifie their chearefulneffe and readineffe for the execution of Gods decrees.

[a] Math.18. 10.& 22.30.
[b] Pfal. 103. 20.21.
[c] Exod.25. 18.&c.
1.king 6.23. and 29.
[d] Ef.6.2.
[e] Exo.25.18
[f] Ef.6.
[g] Ezech.1.

IIII.

The Lord vfeth their minifterie & feruice, both to make relation of his will vnto [a] men, fpecially the [b] godly, (and hence it is they haue their name): & to gouerne [c] the world, in afmuch as they [d] protect the faithfull againft all daungerous euents, the fnares alfo and affaults of their enemies, (which are euill men and Angels,)

[a] Num.22. 32.33.
[b] Gen.19.13 Iudg.13.3.4. 5.Dan.8.16. 9.21.Luke.1. 13,& 26.c.2. 10.Math.1. 20.c.2.13.& 19.20.c.28.5. Act.1.10. Reuel.1.1.
[c] Col.1.16. Ephe.1.22.
[d] Pfal.34.8. 91.11. Gene.14.19.& 16.c.32.1.1.King.19.5.2.King.6.17. & c.19.35. Dan,3.25,& 6.23.

pu-

punifhing [e] the wicked , and [f] chaftening the godly : and for this caufe are they called [g] thrones , dominions , principalities, powers and might.

e Gen. 19 2.
King. 19.35.
Act.12.23.
f 2.Sam. 25.
15.16.
g Ephe.1.21
Col.1.16.

V.

The good Angels are exceeding many, but the number is not expreffed in Scripture.

VI.

When the good Angels were to deliuer any meffage from God vnto mē, they appeared in the likeneffe of [a] young men, very beautifull in fight , and fometimes fhining with fome excellent brightneffe. Somtimes they haue appeared in firie bodies , either like men , as in the vifion of [b] Efay in the Temple : or like horfes and charrets, as in the tranflation or transportation [c] of Elias , and in the protection of Elizeus [d] againft the Syrians . They haue alfo appeared fomtimes when men haue feene them with their eyes [e] waking: and fometimes to men in their [f] fleepe: and fometimes alfo when men watched, but yet ouertaken with fome great [g] afto-

a Gen. 18.2.
and 4.c. 19.
2.Heb.13.2.
Iudg.13.6.
&c.Mar.16.5
Luke.24.4.
Act.1. 10.
b Efay.6.
Ezech.1.
c 2.King 22.
d 2.Kings 6.
e Gen.18.&
19.Luk.1.11.
and 28.
f Math.1.20
g Reu.1.10.

b Luke.1.22
& 24.23.
Act.26.19.
i Act.10.17
19.&11.5.&.
c.16 9.
k Math.17.9
Act.10.3.

nifhment of minde. The firſt kind of theſe apparitions is called in Scripture ὀπλασία, *h* a viſion: the 2. and 3. ὅραμα, a *i* ſight. But yet other whiles the *k* one is taken for the other.

VII.

a Math.28.
3.Act 1.10.
Dan.10.5.&
6.
b Reu.19.10
&.c.22.8.& 9
Col.2.18.
Iud.13.16.

And albeit the good Angels be verie excellent both for maieſtie and *a* glory, yet it is great wickedneſſe to *b* worſhip them, becauſe they are creatures, and our felow-ſeruants.

VIII.

a Pſal.34 8.
& 91.11.12.

The vſe of this doctrine is ; that in dangers we aske of God the protection of the holy Angels : and that we be aſſured, that they ſhalbe ready at hãd for our good according to Gods *a* promiſe.

IX.

a Iohn.8.44.
Iude.6.
1.Pet.2.4.

So farre of the good Angels. The euill Angels are they which by their contumacie and diſobedience againſt God, haue *a* fallen from that bleſſed ſtate or perfectiõ wherein they were created:and ſo become euill : euer ſince maliciouſly inclined to hurt both the glory of God and the faluation of men,

They

X.

They be called in Scripture, euill [a] fpirites, [b] רוחות, horrible, or terrible, becaufe
when they appeared, their very fight did
ftrike fome terror in them which faw thẽ.
And [c] שדים, deftroyers, becaufe they intend
nothing more then the deftruction of mẽ.
And thefe names are found in the old Teftament. And in the new, they are called
[d] δαιμόνια,becaufe of their knowledge to dif-
couer things fecret: and vncleane [e] fpirits,
becaufe they prouoke men vnto all kinde
of filthineffe and vncleaneffe, being mixt
with fuch vnclean mẽ to commit abhomi-
nations. They are alfo called [f] principali-
lities, powers, princes of the world, the
gouernors of the darkneffe of this world,
fpirituall wickedneffes, or euill fpirites,
becaufe they worke mightely in the reprobate.

a 1.Sam. 16.
15.&c.
b Leuit.17.7

c Deut.32.
17.

d Math.9.34
&c.
1.Cor.10.20.
1 Tim.4.1.
Iames.2 19.
Reuel.9 20.
e Math.10.1
f Ephe.6.12.

XI.

The euill Angels alfo are verie [a] many,
but the Scripture fpeaketh not of any certaine number.

a Luke.8.30.

a Iob 1 6.&
c.2.Zach.3.1
Luk.10.1 &
often in the
N. Teftamẽt.

XII.

Their prince is called in Hebrue [a] Sa-

C

than , that is , an aduersarie , becaufe he is
the very enemie of God & his children: &
 Beelzebub , or ᶜ Bahal-zebub , that is ,the
mafter or prince of flies, either becaufe in
Ekron in times paft, that idoll droue away
flies , or had the forme of a flie. In Greeke
his name is ᵈ διάβολος, a deuill, that is, a flan-
derer, becaufe he ᵉ falfly accufeth and char-
geth God & his children for their wordes
and for their workes: and ᶠ ὁ πόνηρὸς, that is a
wicked one , for that he euer goeth about
malitioufly to difturbe the faithfull: and
ᵍ ὁ πειράζων the Tempter, becaufe he temp-
teth Gods people , indeuouring to bring
them to finne and fo to deftruction. He is
alfo called the prince of the world, & that
great Dragon , and the old Serpent . The
reft are called his ᵏ Angels.

b Mat.12.24.
c 2.King.1.2.

d Mat.25.41
Iohn.8.44.
1.Iohn 3.8.
e Iob.1.9.
f Math.6.13
Ephe.6.19.
1 Iohn 3.12.

g Math.4.3.
1.Theff.3.5.
h Ioh.12.31.
& c.14.30.&
16.11.
i Reu.12.9.2
k Mat 25.41
2.Cor.1.7.

XIII.

And albeit Sathan and his Angels bād
themfelues againft God and his children,
& that the deuill oppofe himfelfe as much
as he can in will & defire:yet ean he not ef-
feᷱt any thing,to hurt the faithfull,or a-
gainft the will of God. For the Lordes
power curbeth him , and keepeth him fo
safe

safe bounde that he executeth onely such
things as are᾽ giuen him of God in cōmiſ-
ſion . Neither doth the Lord permit Sathan or his Angels to deſtroy [b] his elect,
but onely to exerciſe [c] them with temptations.

XIIII.

The vſe of this doctrine of wicked ſpi-
rites is , that we may be more watchfull,
to auoide their ſnares and practiſes : and
that we may prouide our ſelues of ſuch ar-
mour as may be ſtrong & of good proofe,
to beate ſo many and ſo ſtrong enemies:
and principally that knowing our owne
ignoraunce and weakeneſſe, we may cry
vnto God for ſtrength, and for protection
againſt all their illuſions & aſſaultes:& as
for weapons to fight with the deuill , they
are without vs , as Gods promiſes & preceptes,or within vs, as faith and prayer,&
obedience to Gods word.

a 1.Kin.22.20
&c.Iob.1.6.
and 2.1.
Math.8.31.
and 32.
b Mat.24.24
Luke.22.31.
32.Io.10.28.
29.33.Ro.8.
35.&c.
c Math.4.1.
&c.
Ephe.6.12.
&c.

CHAP. V.

Of the first integritie of our nature, wherein is entreated of the Image of God, and of free will.

I. APHORISME.

FOrasmuch as after the Angels among Gods creatures, man hath the next place: it is requisite that we learne also in what maner he was created of God in the beginning, that so we may vnderſtād how this our deformitie came not from God in the creatiō, but from some other cause.

II.

a Gene.1.27

Man therefore was created in the beginning after the Image *a* of God; so that he was like the Lord his maker, in that he repreſented his maieſtie in certaine excellent graces.

III.

a Col.3.10. Gen.2.23.

These gifts did appeare partly in ſoule, partly in body. Firſt the ſoule was indued with ſingular *a* wiſedome in the minde or vnderſtanding, whereby he rightly knew both God his creatour, and the workes

or

or creatures of God : next in the will & affection there was a conformitie with the
will of God, and this the Apoftle cals true
righteoufneffe ᵇand holineffe. In the body, *b* Ephe. 4. 24
there did appeare in mans countenance
firft a Princely maieftie , fo as the veric
ᶜ beaftes tooke him for their very Lord or *c* Gene. 1. 28
foueraigne. Some little fparcle of this ap-
peares as yet, for that brute beafts we fee
will be tamed and made tractable to ferue
man, or at leaft wife not to hurt him.

IIII.

Mans will in that firft integritie of nature was free, ᵃ fo as he could thereby *a* Gen. 3. 18.
choofe either good or euill, and therefore
could obey or difobey God.

CHAP. VI.

Of Gods prouidence.

I. APHORISME.

THe prouidence of God, is the eternal,
moft wife, moft iuft, and immutable
counfell or decree of God, gouerning or
difpofing ᵇ euery thing that he hath made
to his owne ᶜ glorie , and the faluation

a Act. 2. 23.
Act. 4. 27. 28.
b Mat. 10. 29
30. Luk. 12. 6.
7. Exod. 21. 1.
Deut. 19. 4. 5.
Prou. 16. laft
v. Heb. 1. 3.
c Prou. 16. 4.
Ro. 9. 11. 13.

d Rom.8.28 ^dof his elect.
1.Cor.11.32

II.

It foloweth therefore that fortune is no cause at all to effect any thing.

III.

a Gen.37.28
and 45.5.7.8.
Ex.7.6 & c.8.
15.2.Sam.12
12.16.& c.10.
11.1.K.22.19
2.Chro.18.18
Iob.1.21.
Ef.10.5.
Ac.2.23. &c.
4.27.28.
b Pfa.5.5 6.7
c Gen.50.20
Prou.16.4.
Exod.9 16.
Rom.9.17.
Rom.8.28.

And albeit God alfo by his prouidence ^adifpofeth of the finnes of men : yet is he no caufe or any authour of finne , becaufe he is not delighted with finne , but rather ^babhorreth it : neither doth he finne , nor can he finne. Againe for that he neither commendeth nor perfwadeth any vnto finne : neither doth he infpire euill into finners, nor conftraine them to finne: but ^cdirecteth all things to a good end.

IIII.

a Math.27.4
Gen.45 3.
Gene 42.21.

b 2.Sa 16.22
c 2 Sa.16. 13.
d Ge.50.20.
Ef.10.7.
e Iam.1.13.
14.15.

f

Men may not therefore excufe their finnes by Gods prouidence : for as for the wicked, their confciences can ^aconuince them of their own naughtines, & they fin not vnwillingly , but rather take pleafure ^bin fin, and are often caried with full fayle ^cthereunto: and haue euer an euill ^dinten-tion : But the godly fall into finne being feduced by an euill ^econcupifcence : and when they haue finned, they acknowledge their

their offence with ⁱdeteſtation.

V.

The vſe or benefite of this doctrine is three fold. Firſt that we may learne ᵃpa-tience in aduerſitie : for that hereby we know that ᵇ God ſendeth not aduerſitie to deſtroy vs, but for our ᶜ good. The ſecond, that in proſperitie we may be ᵈ thankefull vnto God : for that we ſee, it is God, who moueth mens mindes & actions to wiſh and to do ᶜ vs good : or at leaſt wiſe, albeit they doe wiſhe vs euill, yet they can not ᶠhurt vs, but rather doe vs good. Againe we ſee it is he which giueth a bleſſing alſo to things which haue ᵍ no life euen for our good. The third benefite is, that we may be ʰ aſſured, that God will euer be a father vnto vs, both to protect vs from euill & to confer vpon vs all good things.

VI.

We muſt alſo ſo reſt vpon Gods pro-uidence, as that we doe not neglect the meanes, (if we can haue them) but vſe them with reuerence, and in the feare of God, as inſtrumentes ſeruing Gods pro-uidence: not that we ſhould truſt in them,

C iiij

ᶠ Pſal. 51.
Mar. 14. v. laſt.
ᵃ Gen. 45. 4. &c. &c. c. 50. 19. 20. 21. 2. Sam. 16. 17. Iob. 1. 21.
ᵇ Amos. 3. 6. Eſ. 45. 7. 1. Cor. 11. 32.
ᶜ Gen 50. 20 Rom. 8. 28. 1. Cor. 11. 32
ᵈ Gen. 24. 27
ᵉ Gen. 32. 6. & 33. 4 and 39. 4. 21. &c.
ᶠ Exod. 3. 21 12. 35. Gen. 31. 24. Nu. 22. & 23.
ᵍ Luk. 12. 15 Leuit. 26. 26. Eſ. 3. 1. Hag 1 6. 1 Kin. 19. 8.
ʰ 1. Sa. 17. 35 2. Tim. 4. 18.

but leaſt we ʼ tempt the Lord.

CHAP. VII.

Of Sinne.

I. Aphorisme.

a 1ohn.3. 4. Sinne is the ᵃ difference or diſcrepance
between the actiō or nature of man, &
b Rom 3.20 the law of God . And therefore by the law
and 7.7. commeth the ᵇ knowledge of ſinne, that is
by comparing mans life and nature with
the law of God , as when the ſpots of our
faces are knowen, by conſidering the face
in a glaſſe.

II.

Sinne is either, that firſt, or that which
bred of the firſt.

III.

a Gene.3. The firſt ſinne is that fall ᵃ or diſobedi-
Rom.5. ence of our firſt parents in Paradiſe, tranſ-
greſſing Gods commaundement concer-
ning that one forbidden fruit.

IIII.

The ſinne which bred of the firſt , is either originall or actuall.

Origi-

V.

Originall sin is that which is inherent
in our nature from our firſt [a] conception:
to wit , the [b] apoſtaſie of all the naturall
ſonnes of Adam in his loynes , & the corruption of nature that folowed:which the
Apoſtle calleth the ſinne [c] which dwelleth
in vs.

a Pſal.51.7.
b Ephe.2.3.
Rom.5.12.
c Rom.7.20

VI.

This corruption doth moſt infect the
vnderſtanding and the will.

VII.

The vnderſtanding or minde is ſo dark-
ned , that albeit in earthly things , and
things pertaining to ciuill life,it doth diſ-
ſcerne often very much :yet in heauenly
matters,that is , in thoſe things which cõ-
cerne the pure worſhip of God and the
euerlaſting ſaluation of our ſoules , it is
[a] altogether blind.

a 1.Cor.2.14
Iohn.1.5. 18.
c.6.44.c.9.39
Math.16.17.
Act.26.18.
Rom.1.21.22
23.

VIII.

The will is ſo [a] corrupted , that albeit a
man wiſh well vnto himſelfe :yet hath he
no deſire to thoſe things which concerne
the worſhip of God, and his owne ſaluation for euer : but is moſt ſtrongly bent

a Gen.6.5.
chap 8.21.
Rom. 8.7.

to will and defire the contrary.

IX.

Originall finne in refpect of the corruption of nature, either ᵃ raigneth, as appeareth in moft of the vnregenerate: or raigneth not, but is refifted: and this refi-
ftance is either by the onely light of ᵇ naturall reafon, as in the vnregenerate, which
are called continent: or by the working
alfo of the ᶜ holy Ghoft, as in the regenerate.

ᵃ Rom.6. 12

ᵇ Rom.2.14.

ᶜ Rom.8 2.
10.11.

X.

Of originall finne, becaufe of naturall
corruption iffueth finne actuall: which
confifteth in action, as in thought, word,
or deed.

XI.

Actuall finne may be diftinguifhed
many wayes. For firft it is a finne either
of commiffion or omiffion. A finne of cõmiffion is, when any thing is committed,
which is in the law forbidden, as murder,
adulterie, theft. A finne of omiffion is,
when any thing is omitted, which in the
law is commaunded to be done, as when
a man doth not giue due honour to his
parents.

parents.

XII.

Secondly, an actuall finne is committed or omitted either in foule or fpirite onely, or both in body [a] and foule.

a 1.Cor.7. 3. 5.and 2.Cor.7.1.

XIII.

Thirdly actuall finnes, fome are committed againft God, fome againft the neighbour, fome againft our owne felues.

XIIII.

Fourthly, actuall finne is either a notvoluntarie, or voluntary. The not voluntarie, as euill [a] thoughts, and [b] lufts which fteale vpon vs againft our will. The voluntary is, when the will is delighted with wicked lufts, or at the leaft wife fauoureth them. Whereupon againe it foloweth that a voluntary fin is either a full finne, or a broken. A full finne, is when a man with [c] full purpofe, and with all his might rufheth to cōmit things, whereunto wicked luftes driue him. A broken finne I call that, when a man is [d] caried by his euill concupifcēce to confent to do that which he doth not approue. Againe a voluntary finne may be diftinguifhed into finne

a Mat.15 19.
b Rom.7 7. and 8.
Mat.5.12 28.

c Iohn.8.34.

d Rom.7.15 &c.

*Raſh or vn-
aduiſed.
e 1.Sam. 25.
13. vnaduiſed , and deliberate . Sinne vnaduiſed is , when the ᵉ will doth vnad-
uiſedly and ſuddenly conſent and giue
place to euill luſtes . Sinne deliberate is,
when the will doth not haſtely conſent to
f 2.Sam. 11 . euill affections, but with ᶠdeliberation going before.

XV.

* Or open. Fiftly , actuall ſinne is either ſecret or
* knowen . Againe, a ſecret ſinne is either
a Pſal. 19.13 vnknowen to him which committeth ᵃit,
b 1.Tim.5.24 & to others alſo with him: or to ᵇ others it
is ſecret, but knowen to himſelf. A knowē
ſin is either knowen to him which cōmit-
teth it: or knowen alſo to others with him.

XVI.

a Mat. 12.31 Sixtly, an actuall ſin is either ᵃremiſſible
or irremiſſible . Remiſſible is that which
hath repentāce with it : irremiſſible which
wanteth it; & of this kind there is but one,
that ſin which is called the blaſphemie a-
b Ibid. gainſt the holyᵇGhoſt: which is, whē a mā
of deuiliſh malice doth contradict the veritie of the celeſtiall doctrine, againſt the
teſtimonie of Gods ſpirite, which conuin-
ceth him in his cōſcience therof: & yet further

ther proceedeth in a deadly hatred & per-
fecution of the profeffors of the truth, and
this kind of finne Chrift obiected againft
the Pharifies. And Iohn called this finne, a
finne vnto ^c death, and warneth that we
pray not for him which committeth the
fame. The reafon whereof Paul rendreth
in the Epiftle to the Hebrues, in that
he faith; it is ^d impoffible for fuch to be
renued by repentance: for the iuft iudgement of God is againft fuch, who will not
be mocked, neither will he fuffer ^e his fpirite, which is the fpirite of truth, to be
charged with a lye.

_c 1.Ioh.5.16.

_d Heb.6.4.

_e Gal.6.7.

XVII.

And if we admit the old diftinction in
this fenfe, where fin is diftinguifhed into
veniall and mortall, it may well be admitted. But not otherwife, as when they call
that veniall which meriteth pardon, becaufe it is but fmall and light: and that
mortall which meriteth death, becaufe it
is great. For euery finne of his owne nature, euen the leaft, ^a meriteth death:
and not onely temporall death, but euen
^b eternal, Cotrarily all they obtaine pardo

_a Rom.6.4.
laft.

_b 1.Ioh.5.16

which do repent and beleeue in Chrift,al-
beit they haue committed moft greeuous
finnes.

XVIII.

Again a finne pardonable is either the
leffer finne, or the greater. And both are
confidered or iudged either by the principall antecedent working caufe, (which
the Greekes call προηγυμένη,) or by the maner of doing, or by the obiect or matter
wherein the finne is committed.In refpect
of the caufe,the finne is the leffer which is
committed of ignorance, as Paules perfe-
cution; or of infirmitie as the fall of Peter:
but the greater, which is committed a-
gainft the confcience,as Dauids murder
and adulterie : or of malice, as Semeis re-
prochfull and rayling fpeaches . In refpect
of the manner of doing, his finne is leffe,
which offereth adultery by perfwafion, as
Dauid with Bethfhabe , then his finne,
which offereth violence , as that vnclean-
neffe committed with Dina by Sichem,
Iudg.19.   and with the Leuites wife by the men of
Gibeah. In refpect of the obiect, the ftea-
ling of a peny is a leffer finne then of an
hun-

hundred or a thoufand crownes . Againe it is a leffer finne to fteale a beaft, then to fteale a man , which finne they call * *Pla-* * Stealing *gium* in the Latin toung . And it is the lef- either free
fer finne to fpeake an idle word : but the and keeping
greater to fpeake any blafpemie, or any them clofe
thing hurtfull to our neighbour.

in bonds.

XIX.

It appeareth by thefe diftinctions , that finnes are vnequall, contrary to the Stoiks Paradoxe : & this alfo may be vnderftood by the ᵃ vnequalitie of punifhments.   *ᵃ* Mat. 12.15

XX.

And thus farre of the kindes and degrees of finne : The authour of finne firft is the ᵃ deuill deceiuing our firft parentes, *ᵃ* Gene.3.6. next after him our firft ᵇ parentes them- &c.Ioh.8.44. felues , in that they gaue place to the de- I.Iohn.3 8. uils lyes.   *ᵇ* Gene.3.6.

XXI.

The effect or punifhement of finne, is ᵃ death both of body and of foule , both *ᵃ* Rom.8.v. temporall and eternall, and all kindes of laft. ᵇ griefes and miferies.

ᵇ Gen.3.6.
&c.

CHAP. VIII.

Of the law of God.

I. APHORISME.

a Pſal.1.2.
b Exo.20 1.2
c Exod.19.
Iohn.1.17.
Gal.3.19
d Deut.6.6.
Pſ.147.v.laſt
Deut.4 6.7 8
e Pſal.19.8.
Pſ.78.3.& 56

THe law of God is a ᵃ doctrine ſent frō ᵇ God by ᶜ Moſes to the people of ᵈ Iſraell, whereby he teſtified ᵉ and taught in what manner he would be worſhipped of them.

II.

a Rom 9.4.
b Exod.20.
e Leuit.
d Exo.21.22

Of Gods lawes ſome ᵃ are ᵇ morall, ſome ᶜ ceremoniall, and ſome are ᵈ iudiciall.

III.

a Exod.2.22
23.

The iudicials, are lawes of the ᵃ right of contractes, and of penalties for offenders, giuen for the preſeruation of publique peace and iuſtice among men, and for the puniſhment of the contempt of the lawes of God.

IIII.

a Leuit. 1.2.
3.4 6.7.5.

The ceremonials, are ᵃ lawes concerning the ceremonies which God appointed for his externall worſhip, and for the inſtructiō of that people, cōcerning their
euer-

uerlasting saluation by Christ which was
to come.

V.

The morals, are lawes ᵃ concerning the
maners and duties of euery man towards
God and towardes his neighbour.

ᵃ Exod. 20. Deut. 5. 6.

VI.

The morall lawesᵃare disperſed in all the
bookes of Moſes, but in the Decalogue
they are ſummarily collected.

ᵃ Ibid.

VII.

The Decalogue is diuided into two ᵃ Tables: of the which two, the first containeth
foure preceptes, concerning our duties to
God, or concerning the ᵇ loue of God: the
ſecond Table conteineth ſixe preceptes,
concerning our duties to our neighbour,
or how ᶜ to loue our neighbour.

ᵃ Exo. 24. 12 and 31. 18. & 32. 16. & 34. 1

ᵇ Mat. 22. 37 Deut. 6. 5.

ᶜ Ibid. 39. Leuit. 19. 18.

VIII.

Theſe precepts for the moſt part haue
their * Synecdoche: for in the prohibition
of ſinnes, he commaundeth the contrarie
vertues, and contrarily in commaunding
the vertues he doth prohibit the contrary
ſinnes: and by one ſpeciall he vnderſtandeth all of that kinde, or the generall, and

* A trope or figure when part is vn-derſtood by the whole, or the whole by the part.

D

with the externall actions, the internall
thoughtes and luftes muft be vnderftood.
IX.

Furthermore to attaine the right fenfe
& meaning of the Decalogue, thefe rules
alfo muft be obferued. *The meaning of eue-*
ry precept muft be taken, of the end and fcope
for the which that law was giuen, to wit, the
next end: as for exãple. The end of the fift
precept is the preferuation of ciuill order,
& focietie: therfore there are commanded
duties of fuperiours to inferiours, and of
inferiours to fuperiours, for that without
this no ciuill order can be kept. Againe
for diuerfe refpectes, the fame action may be
commended in diuerfe lawes : for the endes
caufe actions to differ: as, protection, as it
is the dutie of parentes towards children,
or of Magiftrates to fubiects, it is cõman-
ded in the fift law : but as it is an office of
Chriftian fortitude in the preferuation of
life, it is contained in the fixt law . So
falfe witneffe, in that it hurteth the good
name of the neighbour, it belõgeth to the
ninth Commandement; but fo farre as it
tendeth to hurt his life, it doth appertaine
to

to the fixth precept.

Againe: *The correlatiues are commaunded with their relatiues: for that the one can
not ſtand without the other*: where therefore it is commaunded in the fift precept
that ſome obey, it is commãded alſo that
ſome doe gouerne: and where the gouernours are commãded to be honored, they
are commãded alſo ſo to liue, as that they
be worthy of honor. So in the fourth precept, where mē are commanded to learne
the word of God, ſome alſo are commanded to teach the ſame. Againe: *The ſecond
Table muſt giue place to the firſt: for we muſt
loue the neighbour for the Lordes cauſe, that
is, for that the Lord commandeth, and to his
glorie.* Therefore parents and all ſuperi-
ours muſt be honoured as is commanded
in the ſeuēth precept of the ſecond Table:
but (as the Apoſtle ſpeaketh) 'in the Lord,   *Epheſ.6.a*
that is, in the feare of the Lord, ſo as the
Lord be not offended, when they be honored.

But this rule muſt be vnderſtood of the
morall law: for in theſe the ſecond Table
muſt giue place to the firſt, but not in the

ceremoniall. If therfore the neceſſitie and life of our neighbour require an omiſſion

b Oſe.6.6. Mat.32.4. & chap.15.3. 4.5.6.

of a ceremonie, we muſt rather[b] omit a ceremonie then neglect the life of our brother. Therefore this rule alſo muſt be kept. *The ceremoniall law muſt giue place to the morall.*

X

a Pſal.147. 19.20. Deut.4.6.7.8

God gaue his law,[a] partly therby (as by a ſpeciall marke) to put differēce between his people and all other nations and people of the world: partly that he might be

b Deut.4.1. &c. & chap. 12.32. *c* Gal.3.23. 24.Heb.9.& 10.

worſhipped by them as himſelf had[b] preſcribed: and partly to prepare them vnto [c] the faith of Chriſt which was to come.

XI.

His preparation was both by inſtruction, and by charge.

XII.

Firſt, he taught them by ceremonies, which were as viſible Prophecies concer-

a Heb.9.& 10.

ning Chriſt,[a] ſhadowing his ſacrifice, wherby he ſhould expiate the ſinnes of all the elect.

XIII.

a Col.2.14. Rom.3.20.

He vrged and charged them, in[a] conuincing

uincing them of finne, both by the ceremonies, and by the law morall, but fpeci-
ally in that by ᵇ by threatning his curfe a- *b* Deu.27.26
gainft them, he caufed them to feeke for Gal.3.10.
grace in Chrift.

XIIII.

Concerning the abrogatiõ of the law,
thus it is; a law is faid to be abrogate, whẽ
it is repealed, made voide, or abolifhed: fo
that the people to whom it was giuen, and
whom it did binde, are no more bounde
thereby.

XV.

Therefore the morall law, may not be
fayd to be abrogate, becaufe it is a perpetuall rule of iuftice cõmanding fummarily *a* Mat.22.40
the ᵃ loue of God and of the neighbour,
which are mens duties for euer. Albeit it
be grãted alfo as true, that the faithful are *b* Gal.3.13.
freed by Chrift frõ the ᵇ curfe, feueritie or, *c* 1.Iohn.5.3
ᶜ extremitie of the law. Rom.6.14.

XVI.

But as for the ceremonial law, that it is *a* Col.2.14.
ᵃ abrogate is euident by the fcope and vfe Ibid. 17.
thereof. For it was giuen to inftruct that Ephef.14.15.
ignorant people as a ᵇ fchoolemafter, con- Gal.3.25.
 b Gal.3.24.

cerning Chriſt to come, and to lead them
vnto him as by the hand, by ſhadowing &

ᶜprefiguring Chriſtes Prieſthood many
wayes. The ᵈ truth then being come , and
we finding the liuely and ᵉ expreſſe image
of all things needful for ſaluatiō in Chriſt:
it foloweth , that theſe legall ſhadowes &
figures are aboliſhed, & that the law hath
performed and ended that pedagogie.

XVII.

The queſtiō is harder cōcerning the a-
brogatiō of the Iudiciall law.For it cā neither ſimply be ſayd to be yet in force, ſeeing the common wealth of the Iewes is a-
boliſhed : neither yet may we ſay that it is
altogether abrogat, for that it containeth
many lawes which haue a ſcope & vſe per-
petuall.It ſeemeth then that this queſtiō
may be thus anſwered.The Chriſtian Magiſtrat is not bound to the Iudiciall lawes
of Moſes in reſpect of ſome ſpeciall circū-
ſtances which did concerne the people of
Iſraell :notwithſtanding concerning the

kindes of ᵃ penalties which the Lord hath
appointed for the reuerend eſtimation &
obſeruation of the Decalogue , the Chriſtian

ſtian Magiſtrats ſeeme to me aſſuredly, at this day to be no leſſe bound for the keeping of theſe lawes, then the Magiſtrates of the people of Iſraell were in elder ages.

CHAP. IX.

Of the likeneſſe and difference of the old and new Teſtament.

I. Aphorisme.

THe word Teſtament is here vſed, to ſignifie the couenãt, which God made with his people.

II.

The cauſe wherefore this word is vſed, is for that the Greeke interpreters of the Bible, trãſlated the word *Berith* (which ſignifieth a couenãt) διαθήκην, a Teſtament: [a] vſing the word (as it ſeemeth) in generall ſenſe, as if they had συνθήκην, a couenant. And for this cauſe the Apoſtle [b] vſeth the word Teſtament in his Epiſtle to the Hebrues, diſputing alſo from the proper ſignification thereof.

[a] 1.King.5.
2.Kings.23.
Eſay.59.
Ierem.31.
[b] Heb.9.15.
16.72.

III.

And aſſuredly the free couenãt of God,

hath this common with a Testament, that it could not be ratified and confirmed but by the *a* death of the parties couenanting, that is, by the death of the sonne of God, who being very God, together with the Father and the holy Ghost, made that his couenaunt of grace with his people.

a Heb.9. 15.
16.17. *a*

IIII.

The Legall couenant also was confir-med by the death of *a* beastes, albeit this were but ceremonially.

a Exod.24.5
6.7.8.
Heb.9.18.
19.20.

V.

The Lordes couenant with his people, is taught in Scripture to be double . The couenant Legall, or of workes; and the couenant Euangelicall or of grace.

VI.

The couenant Legall, is that wherein God in elder ages promised the Israelites all manner of *a* blessings corporall, and also life *b* euerlasting, vnder côdition of yeel-ding *c* perfect obedience to Gods law by their owne *d* strength, and contrarily, he threatned diuerse *e* curses, and eternall *f* death to all such as did breake any *g* one Commandement of the law. The ratifica-tion

a Leuit.26.
Deut.28.
b Leuit.18.5.
Gal.3.12.
Ma.19.16.17
Luke.10.25.
26,27.28.
c Ibid.
d Deut..6.5.
Luke.10. 27.
e Leuit.26.
Deut.27.
f Gal.3.10.
g Ibid.

tion and confirmation of this couenant is
deſcribed. Exod.24.

VII.

The Couenant of grace is that, wherin
the Lord hath promiſed his free [a] fauour
and grace for euer [b] to all them which beleeue in Chriſt: vnder condition of that
[c] bleſſed faith, and true godlineſſe or new
obedience ioyned therewith ; yet neither
of both theſe graces to proceede frō their
owne ſtrength, but to be the meere giftes
of God freely [d] giuen them.

a Gen.12, 1.
2.3 & chap.
15.& c.17.
b Iere.32.40
c Mar.16 16
Iohn.3.16.
Ro.10.9.10.

d Iere.31.33
34.Ephe.2.8.
Iohn.5.25.
Iohn.6.45.

VIII.

Whereas the old and new Teſtament
are oppoſed the one to the other: we muſt
note, that the old Teſtament is taken two
manner of wayes: ſometimes to ſignifie
the Legall [a] couenant, ſometimes to ſignifie the couenant of grace as it was eſtabliſhed with Abraham & his poſteritie. But
by the new Teſtament the couenant of
grace onely is vnderſtood.

a Ierem.31.
31.32.
Heb.8.8.9.
13.& chap.9.
15.18.

IX.

Now if any aske of the likeneſſe & difference of the old and new Teſtament : by
the name of the old Teſtament, we muſt

vnderſtand that couenant of grace , as it was confirmed with' Abraham and all the fathers before the comming of Chriſt. Therefore in this compariſon of both Teſtaments, there is no mention to be made of the Legall couenant.

a Gene.17.

X.

The likeneſſe therefore or agreement of both Teſtamentes doth conſiſt herein, that both haue one and the ſelfe ſame ſubſtance:but they differ in that the miniſtration is diuerſe.

In ſubſtance the ſelf ſame the old and new Teſt. or couenāt: but the miniſtration diuerſe.

XI.

In the ſubſtance of the couenant three things are to be conſidered: The firſt , is, what the ſcope is of the calling of Gods elect: The ſecond,what is the antecedent * mouing cauſe of the couenāt:The third, what the ſtirring , mouing and * meritorious cauſe is.

* The Greekes call it, προηγκμένη: antecedent or principall cauſe.

* The Greekes call this προκαταρτικὴ, the euident cauſe.

XII.

The ſcope of the calling of the fathers and of eſtabliſhing Gods couenant with them, was the bleſſed immortalitie : The mouing cauſe , Gods free fauour & grace in their vocation. The meritorious cauſe was,

was, the death of the mediator.

XIII.

That God propoſed and promiſed to
the fathers not an earthly, but heauenly
beatitude, may appeare by theſe arguments: Friſt, becauſe they were called by
the ᵃpromiſe of the Goſpell, wherein it is
euident that men are called vnto an heauenly ᵇfelicitie. Secondly, for that they
had the ſame ᶜSacramēt with vs, the ſame
I ſay, in ſignification, that is, ſeales of the
ſame grace. Thirdly, for that God vouch-
ſafed to make theſe holy fathers partakers of his word, whereby ſoules are
ᵈquickened, and men are lift vp vnto the
hope of life euerlaſting, Fourthly, for that
God promiſed thoſe fathers that he wold
be their ᵉGod, that is, that he would be not
onely the God of their bodies, but alſo &
principally the God and Sauiour of their
ſoules for euer: and therefore he promiſed
to knit their ſoules vnto himſelfe in righteouſneſſe, that he might make them partakers of life ᶠeuerlaſting. Fiftly, for that
God in his couenant teſtified, not onely
that he was now their God, but alſo pro-

ᵃ Rom 1.2.
Rom.3.21.

ᵇ Ephe.1.13
2.Theſſ.2.14
ᶜ 1.Cor.10.
3.and 4.

ᵈ 1.Pet.1.23

ᵉ Leui.26.12
Math.22.32.

ᶠPſal.144.15
Pſal.33.12.
Haba.1.12.
Deut.33.9.

g Gen.17.7.   miſed that he would be their God for ſe-
uer: in which promiſe aſſuredly the hea-
uenly felicitie & life euerlaſting is plainly
ſignified vnto vs . Sixtly , for that God
promiſed alſo that he would be the God

h Ibid.   of their ſeede after them, that is, of the poſteritie of them after their death, for their
ſake and for their comfort. Seuenthly, for

i Exod.3.6.   that God profeſſed of Abraham, Iſaac &
Math.12.32. Iacob after their death , that he is their
God . Eightly, becauſe thoſe holy fathers
were exerciſed with many and great mi-

k Gene.4.8.   ſeries in this life: whereby it is manifeſt,
Gen.6.7.8.9. that they waited and looked to receiue at
Gene.12.13. Gods hand, not an earthly but an heauen-
&c.
Gene.26.27. ly reſt and happineſſe : otherwiſe they
Gene.28.29. ſhould be fruſtrate of their hope , and ſo
&c.   deceiued by the oracles and diuine promiſes of God . Ninthly, for that Paule
to the Hebrues teſtifieth , that Abraham,

l Heb.11.9.   Iſaac and Iacob , did by faith abide in
        the land of promiſe as in a ſtraunge coun-
trey , looking for, deſiring, and minding
their heritage, and Citie, and countrey in
heauen . Tenthly , for that if theſe fathers had not expected the complement
                              of

of Gods promises in heauen, they had bin more blunt and [m] voyde of vnderstanding then very blockes: for that they so egerly sought after these promises, for the which there could be no hope that euer they should be performed on earth. Eleuenthly, for that those fathers Abraham, Isaac and Iacob [n] confessed that they were strangers in the land of Chanaan: and therefore we must necessarily vnderstand, that the [o] promise made of God vnto them cōcerning that land, may not principally and properly be vnderstood of that land, or of any earthly happinesse to be enioyed in that place, but of life euerlasting, as signified by type and figure. Twelfthly, for that those holy fathers would be [p] buried in the land of Chanaan, to retaine the seale or Sacrament of eternall life which God had giuē thē. Thirtenthly, for it is very apparant, that those holy fathers in all their [q] desires & purposes set euer before thēselues the blessed state of eternall life. Fourteenthly, for that Iacob being euen ready to die, professed that he *expected the*

m 1.Cor.15.19.
n Gen.47.9. Psal.39.13.
o Gen.15.18
p Gene.47.29.30. Gene.50.24.
q Psal.119.166.& 174.

ſaluation of the Lord, that is the Lord had promiſed, and ſhould giue him : and then

ᵣ Gen.49.18 could he not ʳ looke for in this life , becauſe that anon after he died & departed from the ſame . Fifteenthly, for that the Prophets teſtifie, that the couenant made

ſ Eſa 51.6. with the fathers was ˢ ſpirituall, and there-
Iob.19.25.&c fore that life euerlaſting was promiſed vn-
Iohn.13.15. to thē therin. Sixteenthly, becauſe Chriſt
Eſa.66.22.
&c. promiſing eternall life to his Diſciples,
Da.12.1.&c.
ᵗ Math.8.11 ſaith they ſhould ᵗreſt with Abrahā, Iſaac and Iacob. Seuenteenthly , for that Peter

ᵘ Act.3.25. ᵘpromiſing that Euāgelicall benediction, that is, remiſſion of ſinnes and life euerlaſting, to the faithfull Iewes of his time, he made them herein equall to their fathers.

ᵡ Mat. 27.52 Eightenthly. For that Chriſt in his ᵡreſurrection raiſed vp many of the Saints with him vnto life euerlaſting : and therfore, becauſe there is one & the like reaſon of all the elect, the reſt alſo ſhalbe aduanced in due time vnto the kingdome of haeuen. Nineteenthly, for that thoſe holy fathers

ʸ 2.Cor.4.13 had the ſelfe ſame ſpirit of ʸ faith we haue,
Gene.15.6. therefore they were as well as we regene-
Hebr.11. rate vnto the hope of eternall life.

Againe,

XIIII.

Againe it may appeare by the premiſes, that the couenant, whereby the fathers were reconciled vnto God, reſted
not vpon any of their merites, but onely
on the free *mercy of God which called *a* Ioſ.laſt.2.3
them to his grace and fauour : againe it is
manifeſt that they receiued and knew
b Chriſt a mediatour by faith, for by him *b* Heb.11.4.
they were receiued to cōmun with God, Iohn.8.56.
and made partakers of his holy promiſes. Dan.9.17.

XV.

Thus far we haue ſhewed the likeneſſe
and agreement of both Teſtaments : now
it foloweth that we declare alſo how they
differ and diſagree.

XVI.

The difference of both Teſtamentes,
conſiſting in the maner of adminiſtration,
hath foure parts.

XVII.

The firſt difference is this, that the couenant of grace in the old Teſtamēt, that
is, before the comming of Chriſt,& that
glorious appearāce of the holy Ghoſt,was
adminiſtred to *a* Abraham onely with his *a* Gen.15.18
&chap.17.7.

posteritie, and of these principally to the people of the Iewes b the Israelites. But in the new Testament, that is, after the incarnation of Christ, and his Ascension into heauen, the same is administred to other 'nations which came of Abrahams progenie, that is, to the Greekes & d Gentiles 'as Paule speaketh.

b Math.10.5
6.& c.15. 24.
Rom.15.8.
c Mat.28. 19
Mar.16. 15.
Act.9.15.

d Rom.3.29.
e Rom.1.16.

XVIII.

The second difference is, that the couenant of grace before the comming of Christ was couertly and darkely administred, by certaine promises of the Messias, which then was to come and ratifie the couenant, and by b types and ceremonies shadowing & prefiguring Christ to come. But when Christ was come, the dispensation of this couenant was more cleare and more manifested, in the c preaching of the Gospell, and the seales thereof, Baptisme and the Lords Supper: all which are liuely d testimonies that Christ is already come, and hath fully confirmed this holy couenant.

a Gen.18.21
& c.49. 10.
Deut. 18.15.
2.Sam. 7.12.
Psal.2. &72.
&45.
Esa.7.14.
chap.9.6.&
chap.53.
Mich.5.2.
b Gen.15.18.
Heb.10.1.
1.Cor.2.17.
Iohn.19.36.
c Mat.28. 19
Mar.16.15.
and 16.
d Act.1.18.
Math.26.28.
Mar.14 24.
Luke. 22. 20.
1.Cor. 11.25.

XIX.

The third difference is, that before
Christes

Chriſtes incarnation the couenãt of grace was adminiſtred with [a] leſſe efficacie : but after with [b] greater working grace & power of the holy Ghoſt . For albeit the holy ſpirite wrought in the elect vnder the old Teſtamẽt, by thoſe diuine promiſes & ceremonies, but ſpecially by the [c] ſacrifices, ſuch a meaſure of the knowledge of God as was ſufficient vnto their euerlaſting ſaluation, yet he giueth his elect vnder the Goſpell a [d] greater light of knowledge, & ſo a greater meaſure of the true loue of God. That one example of Abrahams faith, the father of [e] all the faithfull, can not diſproue this aſſertion concerning the regular and ordinarie adminiſtration vnder the Goſpell.

[a] Gal.3.24.
& c.4.1.2.3.
[b] Act.2.17.
Iohn.7.38.39

[c] Pſal.51.9.

[d] Iere.3.34.
Eſa.11.9.and
chap.54.13.
Iohn.6.45.
1.Cor.2.10.
1.Iohn.2.10,
and 27.
[e] Rom.4.18.
&c.
Heb.11.17.
&c.

XX.

The fourth difference is for that the adminiſtration of the old Teſtament, was more [a] burdenſome & greeuous becauſe of the multitude of rites and ceremonies, which exceeded in number, charge & labour the ceremonies of our time.

[a] Act.15.15.

XXI.

And whereas God hath now after

E

Chriſtes Aſcenſion abrogate thoſe ſacrifices & ceremonies of the old Teſtament,
we muſt not therefore thinke any change
in him. For he is rightly ſaid to be incon-
ſtant and mutable, which chaungeth his
purpoſe, or doth any thing contrary therunto. But the Lord in abrogating thoſe
ſacrifices,& in preſcribing another forme
of worſhip, hath neither altered his purpoſe, nor done any thing contrary there-
unto.For his ſcope in the ſeruice and worſhip preſcribed in both Teſtaments, is to
bring his eleƈt to the knowledge of their
ſaluation in Chriſt.Neither hath he done
any thing contrary vnto this : but in his
great wiſedome he hath called and doth
conduƈt cōtinually his eleƈt diuerſe waies
to that end he appointed; as he thought
beſt both for thoſe elder ages & for theſe
times vnder the Goſpel. Not vnlike a ſkil-
full Phiſitiō, which cureth not a mā in his
old age with the ſame medicines which
he vſed for his youth: for ſo doing we may
not think him incōſtant for changing his
preſcriptions. For that he wiſely conſide-
reth the diuerſitie of temperature which

is

is in old and young: and ſo reſpecting this
difference he applieth fit remedies, which
therefore neceſſarily, muſt be diuerſe and
not the ſame.

CHAP. X.

Of the perſon and office of Chriſt.

I. APHORISME.

THe knowledge of Chriſt conſiſteth
principally in two things, firſt to
know what his perſon is, ſecondly what
his offices are.

II.

Chriſt, as touching his perſon, in one
& the ſelfe ſame, he is both [a] God & man.
For he is the [b] only begotten ſon of God,
which hath created of the ſeede [c] of the
[d] virgin Mary [e] for him ſelfe, and ſo [f] aſſu-
med or taken, and perſonally and vnchan-
geably knit vnto him ſelfe, the very body
of man, [g] endued with a reaſonable [h] ſoule:
and ſo whithout any change in his diuine
nature, he was made very man in al things
like vnto vs, ſinne onely [k] excepted.

E ij

a Rom.9 5.
1.Iohu. 5.20.
b Iohn.1.14.
c Heb. 2. 16.
Kuke.1.35 42
d Luk.1. 31.
34.35.
e Heb.10.5.
Ioh.1.3.1.10.
4.2.Luk.1.35
f Heb.2.16.
g Heb. 10. 5.
& chap. 2.14.
h Mat.26 38
& c.27 5c.
i Heb.2, 17.
k Heb. 4.15.

III.

This perſonall vnion of two natures in Chriſt, is well demõſtrated by that phraſe or manner of ſpeaking, which old writers haue called *a communitie of proprieties.* And this communitie is nothing elſe but a Synecdoche, whereby we attribute that which is proper to one nature of Chriſt, to the very perſon, hauing his denomination of the other nature. As where Paule ſaith, *ᵃThey crucified the Lord of glory,* ᵇand again, *God hath purchaſed a Church with his own bloud:* & ſo when Chriſt ſpeaketh, ᶜ *no man hath aſcẽded vp to heauen but he which came downe from heauen, the ſonne of man which is in heauen.*

κοινωνία
ἰδιωμάτων,

ᵃ 1.Cor.2.8.
ᵇ Act.20.28.

ᶜ Iohn.3.13.

IIII.

And ſomtimes we haue an expreſſe diſtinction of both natures, as where Chriſt is ſayd, ᵃ *to be made of the ſeede of Dauid according to the fleſh, and declared mightely to be the ſonne of God, touching the ſpirite of ſanctification, by the reſurrection from the dead,* and where he is ſayd, *to* ᵇ *come of the fathers as concerning the fleſh.* So alſo whẽ he is ſaid, *to be,* ᶜ *put to death concerning the*

ᵃ Rom.1.3.
and 4.

ᵇ Rom.9.5.

ᶜ 1.Pet.3.18

the fleſh, but to be quickned in the ſpirite.
And ſometimes this diſtinction is left to
be vnderſtood by conference of ſuch places.

V.

Againe, Chriſt muſt be ſuch a perſon
as is fit to take vpon him the office of a
[a] mediator: And ſuch was none, but the
ſonne of God incarnate: for that he is al-
lied to both the parts which were to be reconciled, and therefore louing both, and
beloued of both. Againe, he muſt ſo performe the office of a mediator betweene
God & vs, that by his [b] death, he reconcile
vs vnto God: and this death being God
only he could not haue ſuffred, and being
man only he could not haue ouercome. A-
gaine, he muſt be very God, that the pro-
pitiatorie ſacrifice (which was his bloud
ſhed for the elect) might be a ranſome &
[c] ſufficient price for our ſinnes : againe he
muſt be very man to [d] ſatisfie the iuſtice of
God: againe a perſon ſanctified of God,
that he might be a holy [e] Prieſt, and a holy
[f] ſacrificer. Againe he muſt be very God,
that (after he had by the merite of his

a 1.Tim.2.5
Heb.8.6.

b Heb.9.15.

c Act.20.28.
1.Iohn.1.7.
d Rom.5.11
&c.
e Heb.7.26.

f 1.Pet.1.19

Priefthood reconciled them vnto God,
and obtained the holy Ghoft for them)he
might alfo him felfe giue them the fame
holy fpirite, to worke faith in them, to receiue him, and his merites.

VI.

The office of Chrift is three fold: for he
is ordained of God to be our Prophet,
Prieft and King.

VII.

He executed his Propheticall [a] functiõ,
or office of a teacher when he was con-
uerfant on earth, in [b] preaching the Gofpell, & reuealing [c] vnto vs the fecret coũ-
fell of God, concerning the great worke
of our faluation by him.

a Deut.18.18
Act.3.22. &
chap 7.37.
b Math 4.17
Efa.61.1.
Luke 4.21.
c Iohn.1.18.

VIII.

He exercifed the office of his Priefthood, partly whẽ he was on earth, & partly doth ftill exercife the fame in heauen.
Whẽ he was on earth, he firft offred prayers [a] to his father for vs, next his [b] owne
body vpon the croffe, and did expiate our
finnes [c] with that his facrifice. In heauen
[d] he appeareth before the face of the heauenly father with his facrifice, once offred

a Iohn 17.
Heb.5.7.
b Heb 7.27.
c Heb.9.25
& c.10.14.
d Heb.9.24.

on

on earth, without^e intermiſſion praying   *e* Heb.10.12
for vs, that the reconciliation we haue
obtained, may be as freſh in memory, and
neuer be loſt.

IX.

The kingdom of Chriſt beginneth in this
life, and is called the kingdome of grace,
and it ſhalbe perfected in the life to come,
which is called the kingdome of glorie.
The kingdome of grace is that ſpirituall
kingdome ^awherin Chriſt ruleth the harts   *a* Ioh.18.37.
of his elect by his word and ſpirite. And
this kingdome he adminiſtred in the old
Teſtament vnto his elect, by Prieſtes and
Prophets, & in the beginning of the new
Teſtament by Iohn Baptiſt, and himſelfe
with his Diſciples: But at the laſt he ſo-
lemnely begā to erect the ſame in the day
of ^bPentecoſt, whē he ſent the holy Ghoſt   *b* Act. 2.
to his holy Apoſtles, that they might go
preach the Goſpell to all nations. So then
he hath euer continued his kingdome on
earth, & ſhall continue it vntill he returne
to iudgemēt, at which time he ſhalbe ru-
ler in the ʿmiddeſt of his enemies: whom   *c* Pſal.110.2.
he plagueth now and then, and deſtroieth,

the laſt he caſt them downe,& make them his ᵈ footeſtoole in his moſt glorious ᵉ cō-ming,at which he ſhall free all his faith-full members from all their afflictions , &

cary them with him ᶠ to heauen,and make them partakers for euer of his heauenly kingdome,which then ſhalbe the king-dome of glorie,when all the Saints ſhalbe tranſlated to heauen,beautified and ador-ned in their ſoules with wiſedome and ho-lineſſe, in their bodies with great excel-lency and immortality, to be with Chriſt, in inſpeakable ioyes and glorie for euer and euer.

CHAP. XI.

Of Faith.

I. Aphorisme.

NOw for that we are made partakers of Chriſtes benefites, which we receiue by his death, as the remiſſion of ſins and

life euerlaſting by ᵃ faith, it ſhalbe expedi-ent alſo that we learne what this faith is, how it breedeth, who receiue this grace, and what proper markes it hath.

This

II.

This faith then, is a fure & firme [a] knowledge of the grace of God, purchafed for
vs by the merites of Chrifts death, and teftified by the word of promife : whereby
euery beleeuer doth apply that promife
of grace vnto himfelfe [b] particularly : affu-
ring him felfe that the fame doth no leffe
appertaine vnto himfelfe then vnto the
reft of the faithfull.

[a] Iohn.17.3.
Rom.8.38.
1.Iohn.3.2.

[b] Gal.2.

III.

The holy [c] Ghoft [a] worketh this faith in
the harts of his [b] elect which are of yeares
by the [d] preaching of the Gofpell.

[c] Mat.16.17
Iohn.3.5.6.8
Ephe.2.8.
Iohn.6.45.

[a] Act.16.14. [a] Iohn.3. 3.5.6.7.8. 1.Cor.4.15. Philem v.10. 1.Pet.1.23.
[b] Iohn.6.37.& chap.8 47.& chap.10.26.Act.13.48.Tit.1.1. 2.Theff.3.
2. [d] Rom.1.16.& chap.10.17.1.Cor.3.5.1.Pet.1.& 25.

IIII.

From this faith arifeth that holy [a] affiance and truft in God whereby the beleeuer refteth himfelfe comfortably in the
fatherly [b] fauour & grace of God purchafed for him by the death of Chrift, confidering both the truth [c] & [d] power of God:
from this affiance do ftreame forth al our
fpirituall [e] ioyes and comforts, and all our

[a] Ephe.3.12
[b] Pfal.32.
[c] Heb.11.11.
[d] Rom.4.21
Heb.11.19.
[e] Iohn.8.56.
Rom.14.17.
Iohn.5.25. &
c.6.57.& 63.

ſpirituall life, according as by it we taſt of ᶠ the great grace and fauour of God.

V.

Againe, from this faith ariſeth, and proceedeth the aſſured hope ᵃ of euerlaſting life, or of the celeſtiall glorie, which we ſhall haue with our Lord Chriſt in his kingdome.

VI.

Againe, from this fountaine ſprings the holy ᵃ inuocation of God, our moſt faithfull and bountifull Father, and our moſt mightie Lord and God.

VII.

Faith alſo cauſeth vs to make a true ᵃ profeſſion : and confeſſe with the mouth to the glorie of God, that which we beleeue with the heart.

VIII.

To be ſhort, hence proceedeth the ᵃ true loue and reuerend feare of Gods children, which cauſeth them with all indeuour to pleaſe, and carefully to auoyde what may offend and diſpleaſe his holy ſpirit.

IX.

The grace of ᵃ perſeuerance is an inſeparable

parable companion of faith : for faith neuer dieth, albeit fometimes it be, as it
were [b] ouerturned, and as buried with the
tempeftes of temptation.

[b] Mark 9.24.
Pfalm 73.

CHAP. XII.

Of Repentance : where alfo is intreated of the life of a Chriftian, and of bearing the croffe.

I. Aphorisme.

SOmetime by the word *Repentance* in
Greeke is fignified & vnderftood[a] fome
forowing for any fact or deed done, whether a man be moued thereby to do well,
or not moued: fometimes alfo it fignifieth
(as the beft Diuines haue noted) to return
to a perfect and right vnderftanding, or to
waxe wife againe : we follow now this later fignification.

[a] Mat.21.29.
& chap.27.3.

[b] Math.4.17.
Act.2.38. Ro.
2.4. 2.Cor.7.
9.10.2.Tim.1
25.

II.

Repentance then is a [a] chaunge of the
minde, which is by nature wicked, and re-
newing of all faculties of the foule, proceeding from a fincere and religious [b] feare
of God; whereby the mind is caried with

[a] Ezec 18.31
Ier.4.1.3.4.

[b] Ierem.4.4,
Act.17: 30.
2.Cor. 7.10.

an earneſt indeuour to do well , and to pleaſe God.

III.

a Ro.6.4 5.6
Ephe.4 22.
23.24.
Col.3.5.6.8.
9.10.
Pſal.34 15.
Eſa.1.16. 17.

Repentance doth conſiſt of two partes: of *a* mortification of the fleſh, or of the old man, and in the quickening of the ſpirit.

IIII.

Repentance may alſo be diſtinguiſhed into ordinarie or common, and extraordinarie or ſpeciall.

V.

The ordinary and common repentance is that, which all men are bound to put in practiſe all the dayes of their life , becauſe of the corruption of nature.

VI.

a 1.Cor. 5.5.
2.Cor.12.21.

A ſpecial *a* repentance is that, which raiſeth as it were frō death, either thē which haue fallen ſhamefully, or in an vnbridled licentiouſneſſe haue giuen ouer thē ſelues to ſin, or haue ſhaken off the yoke of God in ſome ſpeciall apoſtaſie.

VII.

a Pſal. 31.5,

b Pſal.51.

In an ordinary repentance it wil ſuffice that we confeſſe our ſelues vnto *a* God: but an extraordinary requireth confeſſion, *b* ſorow,

row, and deprecation before the ᶜ congre- *ᶜ* ₂.Cor.₂. ₇.
gation , that the Church may be satis- & ᶜ 18.21.
fied , and receiue againe the sinner which
is excommunicate, for any scandale.

VIII.

There is also an extraordinarie repentance of some one whole congregation,
when fearing the Lords corrections to ap-
proch for some general sinnes of the grea-
test part of the people, they striue by prayer, ª weeping and fasting , to turne a- *ª* Ioel.₂.₁₂,
way the wrath of God from them . They
had also in this , in times past , in the
Church of the Iewes , their ᵇsackloth and *ᵇ* Efter.4.3.
ashes. Ierem.6.26.

IX.

The holy Ghost is the cause efficient,
ª or the Lord which worketh in vs vnfay- *ª* Act.11.18
ned repentance. 2.Tim.2.25.

X.

The ª frute and effect which followeth *ª* Math.3.8.
true repentance , is a Christian life : and
this consisteth in forsaking and ᵇ denying *ᵇ* Luke.9.23
our selues , in meditation of the life to
come , and in the right vse of all earthly
blessings.

XI.

The forſaking of our ſelues, partly reſpecteth men, partly and principally it reſpecteth God.

XII.

The forſaking our ſelues which reſpecteth men, conſiſteth partly in 'reuerēcing
them with all Chriſtian modeſtie, partly
in doing[b] good to them with all ſincere affection of heart.

a Rom.12.10.
Philip.2.3.

b 1.Cor.13.4
&c.
1.Tim.1.5.
1 Iohn 3.18.

XIII.

That denying of our ſelues which reſpecteth God, frameth vs with [a]patience to
reſt contented with that ſtate and condition of life, which the Lord ſhall giue vs,
and ſpecially to the [b] bearing of the croſſe.

a Phil. 4. 11.
1.Tim. 6.0.

b Rom. 8.17.

XIIII.

Special motiues to beare the croſſe patiently are theſe following. 1. Becauſe this
is the good[a] will and pleaſure of our heauenly Father, to exerciſe his children in
this maner, as it were, to make good triall
of them. 2. For that[b] Chriſt himſelfe was
to learne obedience by the things which
he ſuffered, and we muſt be made[c] confor-
mable vnto him. 3. For that if we be[d] partakers

a Heb.12.5.

b Heb. 5.8.
& chap.12 2.
1.Pet.2.21.
c Rom. 8.29.
d Rom. 8.17.
2.Tim. 2.12.

takers with Chrift in his paffions,we fhall
be partakers alfo with him of his glorious
refurrection. 4. For that it is needfull and
good for vs alwayes to haue fome croffe,
that hauing experience of our own weak-
neffe and frailtie, we may be truly ᵉ hum- *ᵉ Pfal.119.71*
bled : that fo being humbled, wee may
learne to call for ᶠ ftrength from God,that *ᶠ 2.Cor.1.9.*
fo we may haue experience of his ᵍ pre- *ᵍ Rom.5.4.*
fence, and that by this experience we may
receiue ʰ confirmation of our hope. 5. For *ʰ 2.Cor 1.10*
that we haue need to learne the obedience *Rom.5.4.*
ⁱ we owe to God, that the rage of our cor *ⁱ Pfal.119.71*
rupt nature be fubdued and bridled, and
that the finnes we haue commited, may
be punifhed, left we be ᵏ damned with the *ᵏ 1.Cor. 11.*
world. 6. For that when we fuffer perfecu- *32.*
tion for righteoufneffe fake, and fpecially
for defence of the Gofpell, we are not only not miferable, but alfo bleffed and hap-
pie, by the ˡ teftimonie of Chrift himfelfe. *ˡ Math. 5.10.*
All thefe reafons,as the matter requireth, *1.Pet.3.14.*
are fpeciall ftrong motiues vnto patience
vnder the croffe.

XV.

True patience is not to want either fenfe

a Ioh.16.20.
& c. 21.18.
εἰαιϑησία.
ἀπάϑηα.
b 2.Cor.4.8.9
ᵃ or naturall affection, and so to be voyde
of all griefe and sorow : but herein appeareth it, when the seruaunt of Christ, is
much ᵇ prouoked, and yet by Gods feare is
so bridled, that he breakes forth into no

c Psal. 39.
rage nor ᶜ murmuring, but rather resteth,
d 2.Cor.6.10
(albeit smitten with griefe & sorow,) ᵈ spiritually comforting himselfe in the Lord
his God : not without meditations also of
Gods iustice, equitie and clemencie in
our chastisements, but specially of the fa-
e Rom.8.28.
1.Cor.11.32.
therly counsell ᵉ of God for our saluation,
so caring for it on this manner.

XVI.

Now the meditatiõ of the life to come,
which is the second part of a Christiã life,
is such, that it carieth with it a contempt
a Phil.1.23.
2.Cor.5.2.
Rom.7.24.
and a lothing of this ᵃ present life, according to the measure of illumination and
knowledge, which God hath giuen vnto
b Eccle.1.1.
c Gene.47.9
d Rom.7.24.
vs, both of the ᵇ vanitie of this present life
by our continual ᶜ miseries, and of the corruption ᵈ of our nature by our dayly trans-
gressions, and according to the measure
of tast, which the holy Ghost hath giue vs
e Rom.14.17
of the glory and ᵉ ioyes of the life to come.
And

XVII.

And yet we muſt not hate this preſent life, becauſe it is one of Gods [a] bleſſings, and ordained of God for our ſaluation: partly for that herein the Lord giueth vs a [b] taſt of his goodneſſe by manifold bleſſings, partly for that by many temptations he prepareth vs for the [c] crowne of the celeſtiall glory.

[a] Exo.20.12

[b] Pſal.34.9.

[c] Tim 4.8.
2.Theſ.1.67.
Act.14.22.

XVIII.

The laſt point is, that the right vſe of earthly bleſſings (which is the third part of Chriſtian life) conſiſteth herein. Firſt, that we vſe this [a] world as if we vſed it not: vſing and receiuing the bleſſings of God for the ſuſtentation and [b] refreſhing of our bodies, but with ſobrietie [c] and [d] thankes giuing. Next, that we beare patiently and [e] thankefully the penurie and wants of earthly things: and that we euer thinke of this, that we muſt render [f] an account vnto God, of the diſpenſation or charge committed vnto vs, and therefore that we vſe the good bleſſings of God temperatly, modeſtly, ſoberly, diſtributing to the neceſſitie of our poore brethren liberally: &

[a] 1.Cor.7.29
30.31.
[b] Pſal.104.15
[c] Rom.13.14
[d] 1.Tim.4.3
45.
[e] Phil.4.12.
[f] Luke.16.2.
Rom.14.10.
and 12.
2.Cor.5.10.

F

laſtly that we containe & keepe our ſelues
within the limites of our calling.

g 1.Pet.4.15
1.Cor.7.17.
1.Theſſ.4.11

CHAP. XIII.
Of Iuſtification.

I. APHORISME.

IF the queſtion be how a man is iuſtified
before God: To iuſtifie doth ſignifie as
much as to acquite, diſcharge or abſolue
in Latin, ſo far as that word ſignifieth the
action of a iudge. A mā is ſaid therfore to
be iuſtified before God, which is accounted iuſt in Gods Iudgement, and accepted
before God for his righteouſneſſe.

a Prou.17.15
Deut.25.1.
Rom.8. 33.
34.& c.5. 18.

II.

A man is ſayd to be iuſtified by his
workes, when in his life there is founde
ſuch puritie and holines, which may merite before the throne of God the commendation of iuſtice: or that can, with the
perfection of his workes anſwer and ſatisfie the iudgement and iuſtice of God.

III.

A man is ſayd to be iuſtified by faith,
which renouncing the righteouſnes of his
workes doth apprehend by faith the righteous

teouſnes of Chriſt, that is, the righteouſneſſe which is purchaſed by the death of
Chriſt; & this mā ᵃclothed with this robe   *ᵃ* Gal. 3. 27.
of Chriſt doth appeare not as a ſinner, but   Apoc. 7. 14.
as a righteous man in the ſight of God.

IIII.

We ſay with the Apoſtle ᵃPaule that a   *ᵃ* Rom. 3. 28.
man is iuſtified before God, not by works   Gal. 2. 16.
but by faith onely.

V.

Iuſtification and regeneration go euer
ᵃtogether, but yet muſt be diſtinguiſhed.   *ᵃ* Rom. 6. 3.
For regeneration in this life onely is ᵇbe-   and 8.
gun, and by degrees increaſeth, till it be   *b* Rom. 7.
perfected in the life to come: but we are
not iuſtified in part, but perfectly: for this
quieteth our conſciences, ᶜand giueth vs   *ᶜ* Rom. 5. 1.
that peace which paſſeth vnderſtanding.

VI.

S. Paule doth well expreſſe this difference betweene iuſtification and regeneration. For ſpeaking of his inherent righteouſneſſe or integritie, which he had in
regeneratiō, he crieth out bitterly: *ò wret-*
ched ᵃman that I am, who ſhall deliuer me   *ᵃ* Rom. 7. 24
from this body of death! But turning him

ſelfe to the righteouſneſſe of Chriſt imputed vnto him(which is grounded vpon
the meere mercy of God , and giuen vs in
b Rom.8.33. our iuſtification)he reioyceth [b] greatly,&
34.35.&c.   with full truſt and affiance triumpheth o-
uer life and death, reproches and wantes,
ſword and all croſſes of this preſent life.

VII.

When we ſay we are iuſtified by faith:
our meaning is that we are pronounced
iuſt in Gods ſight , for that by faith the
a Rom.5.19. Lord doth [a] impute vnto vs for righteouſ-
b Heb.2.9. neſſe, [b] the obedience of Chriſt, which he
c Gal.2.13. performed for vs ,vnto his father, [c] in ta-
Eſa.55.   ſting death for vs,and ſo in paying the [d] pu-
d Rom.4.3. niſhment we did owe for the breach of
&c.
Gal.3.6.   the law.

VIII.

When we ſay we are iuſtified by faith
a Rom.3.24 onely , we do not exclude the [a] grace and
& chap.5.21
Ep.1.5.6.7.8. mercy of God in our iuſtification: nor the
b Rom.3.25. [b] merite of Chriſtes death,which is impu-
& c.5.9.and
c.8.33.34. ted vnto vs for righteouſneſſe : but we ex-
c Rom.3.28. clude [c] workes onely.
& chap.11.
11.6.32.
Gal.2.18.

IX.

For aſſuredly , the iuſtice of faith and
workes

workes are ſo oppoſite , that they can not
be coupled together:but admit the one,ye
muſt neceſſarily reiecte th other . And
hence it is that Paule doth account the
righteouſneſſe of the Law and this righteouſneſſe of faith as contraries, [a] renoun- *a* Phil.3.9.
cing that righteouſneſſe by the law , and
reſting in that righteouſneſſe which is by
faith in Ieſus Chriſt , or giuen vs of God
by faith.Againe, he ſheweth that this was
the cauſe of the [b] ruine of the Iewes, that *b* Rom.10.3.
ſeeking to ſtabliſh their owne righteouſ-
nes,they wold not ſubmit theſelues to the
righteouſneſſe of God . This he teacheth
alſo when he ſaith, that our reioycing can
not be [c] excluded by the law , but by faith: *c* Rom.3.27.
and againe; when the reward is giuen [d] for *d* Rom.4.4.
works,that is of due debt,but that righte- and 5.
ouſneſſe is imputed to faith,is of grace.

X.

Againe Paule doth not exclude from
iuſtification thoſe workes only , which the
vnregenerat work out of grace literally, &
by ſtrength of their own free will:for ſure-
ly Abraham was regenerate, when he did
thoſe workes for the which he had [a] praiſe *a* Rom.4.2.

of men, but was not iuſtified with God.

XI.

To be ſhort , the Scripture teacheth
that our iuſtification is on this manner,
a Tim.3. 5.   firſt the Lord God of his meer' grace and
Ephe.1.5,6.7 goodneſſe doth embrace a ſinner; finding
nothing to moue him to mercy, but miſe-
b Ephe.2.1. ry;for he ſeeth him deſtitute & void of all
c Ephe.1.9. good workes : he is moued ' of himſelfe to
do him good,and to giue this ſinner ſome
d Rom.5.5. taſt and feeling ᵈ of his goodneſſe : that
e Phil.3. 8. ᵉ diſtruſting his owne ſtrength and works
he may repoſe all his truſt and hope for
f Ephe.1.7. ſaluation in the onely mercy ᶠ of God in
Chriſt Ieſus, which God hath reuealed in
his holy word.

XII.

Againe that a mã is iuſtified by faith only, is very cleare by other places of the A-
poſtle: as where he diſputeth that there is
a Rom.4.2. ᵃ no righteouſnes by faith, but that which
3.4.
b Rom.3.21. is by grace: where he ᵇ denieth righteouſ-
and 28.
Gal.2.16.   neſſe to the workes of the law : to workes
(I ſay)not onely ceremoniall but alſo morall : as may plainly appeare by theſe ſen-
tences which he vſeth for confirmation of
his

his purpoſe: as, *the ᶜ man that ſhall do theſe*   c Gal.3.12.
things, ſhall liue in them: and ᵈ curſed is eue-   d Ibid.10.
ry man, that continueth not in all things
which are written in the booke of the law to
do them: and by theſe concluſions: *righte-*
ouſneſſe is not by the law, for by the law com-
meth the ᵉ knowledge of ſinne. The law ᶠcau-   e Rom.3.20
ſeth wrath, Ergo *not righteouſneſſe.*   f Rom.4.15

XIII.

We graunt with Paul that no faith iu-
ſtifieth but that which worketh by ᵃ loue: a Gal 5.6.
but we vtterly deny that faith hath power
to iuſtifie, or that faith and loue do iuſtifie, becauſe faith is effectuall, or working
by loue.

XIIII.

The forme of our iuſtification is the
free remiſſion ᵃ of ſinnes : for like as the   a Rom.4.6.
wrath of God is vpon all ſo long as they   7.8.
continue in ſinne: ſo whom the Lord ſhall   Luke.18. 13.
receiue to grace, them he is ſayd to iuſti-   and 14.
fie, that is, of ſinners to make them righte-   Act.13.38.
ous, & this he doth by pardoning and diſ-   and 39.
charging them from their ſinnes . For if
we conſider them whom God receiued to
his grace by their workes , they ſhalbe

b Rom.9.
1.Iohn.1,8.

founde [b] finners as yet, which notwithſtā-
ding are and muſt be acquited and freed
from their ſinnes.

XV.

Againe thus; the forme of our iuſtification is this: God doth remoue our ſins
from vs and imputes them vnto Chriſt,
and againe imputes the righteouſneſſe of
Chriſt vnto vs: conſider this demonſtra-
tion for thy better vnderſtanding.

God impu-
ting vnto { 1. Guiltineſſe.
Chriſt the { 2. Diſobedience. } Of the beleeuer, cauſe of
his death.
{ 3. Corruption.

God impu-
ting vnto
the belee- { 1. Paſſion.
uer the be- { 2. Righteouſnes. } Of Chriſt,
nefits of the { 3. Holyneſſe. } cauſe of his
life.

a Rom.3.24
25.
Ephe.1.7.
1.iohn.2.1.
and 2.
b Rom.5.19
Phil.2.8.

XVI.

The cauſe which moueth Gods mercy
in our iuſtification is the [a] ſatisfaction and
merite of Chriſt, that is, his [b] obedience
vnto

vnto his father in his ^c death for vs : & this   *c* Heb.2.9.
obedience is ^d imputed vnto vs for righte- *d* Rom.4.6.
oufneffe, that is, is accounted ours, as if
we had performed the fame our felues.

XVII.

And to the end that this obedience and
righteoufneffe of Chrift might be imputed vnto vs : it was neceffarie firft that he
fhould yeeld perfect obedience to the law
of God himfelfe, liuing thereafter in all
holyneffe of life. And to performe this, it
was neceffarie alfo, that he fhould be fanctified & without fin from his beginning,
& firft conceptiõ in his mothers wombe:
for if he had not bene a holy ^a Prieft, and *a* Heb.7.26.
a ^b holy facrificer, he could not haue plea- *b* 1.Pet.1.19
fed God: and fo could not haue pacified
him for vs. And yet further I ad, that this
our high Prieft, and mediator, muft be ve-
ry ^c God, that the obedience of his death *c* Act.20.28
might be of price fufficient for our finnes, 1.Iohn.1.7.
and meet to giue vs an euerlafting righteoufneffe.

XVIII.

The doctrine of our free iuftification,
fhall then be comfortable and pleafant

vnto vs: when we fhall prefent our felues
as guiltie before the heauenly iudge, and
fhall proftrate our felues, and ftrip our
felues as naked in his prefence, full of
feare and care, to be difcharged from our

a Efa.33.14.
b Iob.4.17.
18.19
c Pfal.19.13
Iob.15.16.

fins, confidering the *a* perfection of Gods
iuftice and the *b* imperfection of our righteoufneffe, yea the huge *c* number and
greatnes of our finnes. For thus come we
at the laft, well prepared and ready to receiue the grace of Chrift, when we fhalbe
truly caft down & humbled with the liuely touch and feeling of our miferie and

d Luk.18.11
12.13.14.

wants. But contrarily, fuch as either *d* fwell
in the conceite of their owne righteoufneffe, or be drunke in the delights of their
owne fins, they liue in a fecure contempt
of Gods iudgement, and fhut vp againft
themfelues the gates of Gods mercy.

a Rom.3.19
and 25.
1.Cor.1.30.
and 31.
Ephe.1.12. &
14.& chap. 2
v.8.8. 9.
b Rom 5.1.
& c.8.35.
Ephe.3.12.

XIX.

Furthermore, if we admit not this doctrine of free iuftification: we fhall rob
God of his full *a* glory, and our poore confciences, of founde peace *b* and reft before
his tribunall feate of iuftice: both which
notwithftanding muft be had, & granted.

And

XX.

And we muſt further note that the whole
courſe of our iuſtification is by grace, and
for our better vnderſtanding in this point,
conſider of foure ſortes of men. The firſt is
of them which are neither inwardly nor
outwardly called : the ſecōd ſort is of thoſe
contemners, whom they commonly call
Epicures, which haue an outward but not
an inward calling : the third ſorte is of hypocrites, which deſire ſome commendation of iuſtice by ſome ſhew of externall
workes, but ſpecially by the ceremonies
which appertaine to Gods worſhip : theſe
alſo haue their outward, but not their inward calling : the fourth ſort of men, are
they which haue both an outward and inward calling, whom Gods ſpirite doth regenerate by the Goſpell: and like theſe are
none of the three former kindes.

XXI.

That the firſt kinde haue no righteouſneſſe, but be meer vniuſt and impious before God, hauing alſo no ſtrength to do
that which is good, and to beleeue the
promiſe of grace, is very manifeſt euery

where in Scripture:as when al the ſonnes of Adam are deſcribed in theſe wordes: that they haue ªwicked & rebellious harts, that all the ᵇimaginations of their hart are only euill côtinually,that their ᶜthoughts are vaine,that they haue no ᵈfeare of God before their eyes,that not one of them doth ᵉvnderſtand or ſeeke after God. A-gaine that when God doth enlighten vs with his knowledge, he raiſeth vs from ᶠdeath to life, & makes vs new ᵍcreatures: that we be deadly and ʰprofeſſed enemies vnto God before he receiue vs to grace in our iuſtification :that we haue not loued ⁱhim before he loued vs : that we be not purged from our vncleaneſſe by the bloud of Chriſt, till the ᵏholy Ghoſt worke our inward ſanctification : that then we begin to paſſe from death to life, when through Chriſt we receiue ˡgrace to beleeue.

a Iere.17.9.
b Gene.6.3.
& chap.8.21.
c Pſal.94.11
d Pſal.36.1.
e Pſal.14.2.

f Iohn.5.25.
g Ephe.2.10
h Rom.5.6.
7.8.

i 1.Ioh.4.10

k 1.Cor.6.11

l Phil.1.29.

XXII.

Now for the ſecond and third kinde, that they haue no iuſtice to ſtand before God, may appeare alſo manifeſtly, for that the vncleaneſſe of their owne conſciences is proofe ſufficient that they be not

as

as yet regenerate by the holy Ghoſt, and
this alſo bewrayeth their want of faith.
Whereby it appeareth that they be not as
yet reconciled vnto God, nor iuſtified before him, for that this grace none can attaine vnto, but by faith.

XXIII.

The hypocrites chalenge ſome iuſtice,
becauſe of their glorious workes and obedience to the ceremonies, but they are ſo
farre from pleaſing God herein, that they
highly diſpleaſe him, becauſe with vncleane harts they prophane his holy wor-
ſhip. For workes can not ᵃpurchaſe grace   *a* Hag. 2.12.
with God for any perſon: but contrarily,   13.14.15.
workes pleaſe God, after that the perſon   Eſa.1.11.12.
firſt hath founde fauour and grace with   13.14.15.
God. And for this cauſe Moſes writeth,   Prou.15.8.
that *the Lord reſpected*ᵇ*Abell and his of-*   *b* Gene. 4.4.
fring: in which wordes he teacheth that
Abels oblation did therefore pleaſe God,
becauſe Abels perſon pleaſed him : and
that pleaſed him by faith, without *which*
ᶜ*it is impoſſible to pleaſe God,*for that therby   *c* Heb.11.6.
mens harts are ᵈpurified. For which cauſe   *d* Act.15.9.
alſo Paule ſaith to the Hebrues that Abel

Heb.11. 4. ᶜ offred vnto God a better facrifice then Cain: for that Cain was an hypocrite, and fo without faith.

XXIIII.

Laftly for the fourth kinde, albeit man regenerate by Gods grace haue fome *a 1.Cor.4 4.* ᵃrighteoufneffe of workes : yet the fame is not fuch, nor fo perfect, as that it can ftād before the iudgement feate of God: be- *b Rom 7. 14. &c.* caufe all their good works are ᵇimperfect, and ᶜ polluted with corruptions, and their *Phil.3.13.14 c Efa.64 6. d Eze.18.24.* finnes following do ᵈ bury all the remembrance of their former righteoufneffe and good life.

XXV.

By the premiffes we now fee that not onely the beginning of our iuftification is by grace, fo as a finner freed from damnation obtaineth righteoufneffe, and that freely by the pardon of his finnes, as appeareth in the three firft forts of men:but alfo our proceeding therein, fo as our iuftification is euer free and by grace:which thing well appeareth in the fourth kinde of men which are both, regenerate by Gods fpirite, and iuftified by a liuely faith

in

in Chrift . And thus God imputed vnto
Abraham, the father of the faithfull, his
faith for righteoufneffe, when as he had
ªliued for many yeares in great holyneffe
of life . This faith Habacuk alfo; ᵇ *The iuft*
shall liue by faith : and Dauid; ᶜ *Bleffed are*
they whofe iniquities are forgiuen, fpeaking
of the godly which liue a holy vnfpotted
and blamelefle life before men . Againe
Paule faith that the ᵈ embaffage concerning our free reconciliation with God
muft be continued among the faithfull.
And Chrift is a ᵉ continuall mediator, re-
conciling vs with his father, and the efficacie or vertue of his death to ᶠ expiate the
finnes of the faithfull neuer dieth, nor wa-
xeth old.

ᵃ Gene. 15.6
ᵇ Habac.2.4.
& Pfal.32.1.

ᵈ 2.Cor.5.20

ᵉ 1.Iohn.2.1.

ᶠ Ibid.2.

XXVI.

And whereas the Schoolemen alfo fay,
that good workes haue no fuch vertue in
them, to be fufficient vnto iuftification:
but that their merite & vertue to iuftifie is
by grace: we muft learne that there is no
grace to worke our iuftification, but that
only which moueth God in Chrift to embrace vs, and to iuftifie vs by the merites

of his obedience and satisfaction for vs.

XXVII.

For God accepteth not our workes, but
so farre as we please him, hauing put on
by faith the righteousnesse of Christ, that
is, which Christ purchased by his death for
vs, as is ᵃ before shewed . Neither can
works iustifie in part before God: for God
admitteth no righteousnesse of workes,
but that ᵇ full and perfect obedience to
his law.

ᵃ Aphor.23.

ᵇ Deut.27.26
Leuit.18. 5.

XXVIII.

When they glory of workes of supere-
rogation , whereby they say full satisfaction is made for trespasses and sins committed : how can they answer that saying
of Christ ? ᵃ *VVhen ye haue done all these*
things which are commanded you, say we are
vnprofitable seruants : we haue done that
which was our dutie to do.

ᵃ Luk.16. 10

XXIX.

To be short concerning workes, take
heed of two things : first put no trust in
them, next ascribe no glory to them.

XXX.

The Scriptures driue vs from all confidence

dence in them, teaching vs that all our righteouſneſſe,[a] ſmels in the ſight of God as filthie clouts, and onely prouoke Gods wrath againſt vs. Now take away this confidence of workes, all glorying muſt fall to the ground: for who will aſcribe any commendation of iuſtice vnto workes, if confidence in them cauſe him to tremble in the ſight of God?

XXXI.

Moreouer if we conſider all the cauſes of our ſaluation, we ſhall finde the grace of God to ſhine bright in euery one of them, excluding the righteouſneſſe of our workes. For the authour of our ſaluation is God, the Father, Sonne & holy Ghoſt. The Father firſt, in that[a] of his meere[b] grace & free loue, he ſent his ſonne vnto vs, to redeeme vs from the dominiō of the deuill. Next the Sonne, in that of his free loue[c] towards vs, he became[d] obedient to his father vnto the death of the croſſe, and ſo hath ſatisfied[e] the iuſtice of God for vs. Laſtly the holy Ghoſt, in that he giueth vs[f] faith, whereby we apprehend the iuſtice which Chriſt hath purchaſed for vs by his

a Tit.3.5.
b Iohn.3.16.
1.Iohn.4.9.
and 10.

c Rom.5.7.8
1.Iohn.3.26.
d Rom.5.19.
Phil 2.8.
e Rom.3.25.
1.Iohn.2.2.
f Ephe.2.8.
& chap.1.13

G

death . The end alfo, the Apoftle faith, is
the manifeftation of Gods iuftice , and
the prayfe of his goodneffe.

g Rom.3.25.
h Ephe.1.12

XXXII.

And whereas the Saintes commend o-
therwhiles their innocencie and integrity
before God : this they doe not to the end,
to truft in the iuftice of their workes in
Gods iudgement , and to reft their confciences as vpon a good foundation : but
either to teftifie the goodneffe of their
cauſe againſt their aduerſaries , or to cō-
fort themfelues concerning their adoption, by the fruites of their faith and calling: for that they reft on the onely fauour
of God in Iefus Chrift.

a Pfal.7 9.
Pfal.18.21.
b 2.King 20.3
1.Tim.4.7.8.

XXXIII.

Againe , whereas the Scripture faith,
that the good workes and obedience of
the faithfull doe caufe the Lord to raine
down many bleffings vpon them:we muft
vnderftand,that good workes are fo farre
caufes of Gods bleffings vpon vs , as the
Lord by his former graces, taketh occa-
fion , to giue vs more graces : where note,
that they be not meritorious caufes , but
motiues

motiues onely for ſpeciall graces of Gods
ſpirite going before: for whom the Lord
will glorifie, them firſt he ᵃ ſanctifieth:that ᵃ Ephe.5.26.
their corruption and wickedneſſe may not   27.
hinder their glorification. In a word(as
Auguſtine hath well ſpoken) God crow-
neth the workes of his owne hand in vs.

XXXIIII.

Againe, that our workes do not merite
the grace of God, may yet further appeare
by theſe reaſons folowing. Firſt for that
they are full of ᵃ corruption: next for that ᵃ Eſa.64.6.
they are duties we ᵇ owe vnto God: third- ᵇ Luk.17.10.
ly for that they are not ours, that is, ſuch
as come from the ſtrēgth of our free will,
but the effects ᶜ and fruites of Gods grace ᶜ Rom.8.10.
in vs.   Ephe.2.10.

XXXV.

And whereas good workes pleaſe God
and haue a ᵃ reward, it is not for any me- ᵃ 2.Tim 4.8.
rite, but for that Gods ᵇ goodneſſe doth ᵇ Eſa.55.1.
accept of them and reward them, of his
meere grace and mercy in Ieſus Chriſt.

XXXVI.

Surely no Chriſtian doubteth, but that
we muſt hold faſt, the groundes of Chri-

ftian Religion, and this is a fundamentall point or ground of Chriſtiā doctrine, that Chriſt is giuen 'vs for our righteouſneſſe, or iuſtification: if this doctrine ſtād, the iuſtice of our merites and workes, being a flat contrary, can not ſtand.

a 1.Cer.1.30 and c.3.11.

XXXVII.

There are two opiniōs of Popery which are moſt oppoſite to that great ground of Chriſtiā veritie. The firſt is, that there are ſome moral vertues or works which make men acceptable before God, before they be grafted into Chriſt: the ſecond that Chriſt hath merited for vs, the firſt grace: that is, an occaſiō of meriting with God: & that then it is our parts, to take the occaſion when it is offered.

XXXVIII.

To conclude, we muſt very circumſpectly ſee to this, that we build wiſely vpon that foundation: for that doctrine is found concerning good workes, which is deriued from the doctrine 'of faith, folowing the ſame as the effect doth the cauſe. For to this end are we iuſtified by faith in Chriſt, that we may ſhewe our ſelues

a This is the method which Paule vſeth. in a matter, in all his Epiſtles, as to Rom. Gal.Ephef. Phil.Col.&c.

ſelues thankfull vnto God for ſo inſpeakable a benefite, by our continuall ende-
uour and care to ſerue God in all good
workes, and in all holineſſe & righteouſneſſe of life.

CHAP. XIIII.

Of Chriſtian libertie.

I. Aphorisme.

BEcauſe that Chriſtians, and the faithfull vnder the Goſpell, are freed[a] from
the law: it foloweth now that we conſider,
how farre this Chriſtian libertie is exten-
ded, and wherein it conſiſteth, leaſt any do
wickedly abuſe[b] the ſame againſt the glory of God, his owne ſaluation, and the ſaluation of his brethren.

a Rom. 6. 14.

b Gal. 5. 13.

II.

Chriſtian libertie hath three partes: to
wit, our freedome and diſcharge from the
* iuſtification of the law, from the dominion of ſinne, and from the ceremonies of
the law.

* Or condé-
natió of the
law.

III.

The firſt part of Chriſtiā libertie is this,

G iij

that the conſciences of the faithfull, are freed and diſcharged, from the ᵃ iuſtification of the law, that is, from the neceſsitie of perfect obedience to the attaining of the legall iuſtice, & ſo conſequently from that care and trembling, becauſe of the heauie curſe and wrath of God, which foloweth the breach of the law.

ᵃ Gal.3.13. and c. 5.1.

IIII.

But no man may therefore conclude, that the law is not neceſſary for the faithfull : for, they are euer ᵃ taught, admoniſhed, and moued therby vnto euery good worke: albeit, it can not charge their conſciences, before the tribunall ſeate of God.

ᵃ Rom.7.12.

V.

The ſecond part of Chriſtian liberty is, that Chriſtians are freed from the kingdome ᵃ and dominion of that ſinne & corruption which dwelleth in them, ſo that henceforth they do no more hate nor flie from the law of God, but are delighted therin, becauſe of Gods holy ſpirit which dwelleth in them.

ᵃ Iohn.8.34 36. Rom.6.14.& c 7.22. and chap.8. 2. 1.Iohn.5.3.

This

VI.

This bleſſed freedome, yeelds two benefites: the firſt is a holy truſt and affiance
in God, that their ¹ obediéce, hauing ma-　*a* Malach. 3.
ny wants, yet is acceptable vnto God: the 17.
ſecond benefit, is a chearefulneſſe in per-
forming our duties vnto God, and this foloweth the former immediatly, as the effect the cauſe: & theſe two points are very
pertinent to Gods holy worſhip.

VII.

The third part of Chriſtian libertie is,
that the conſciences of the faithfull, are
diſcharged & freed from the ¹ ceremonies　*a* Gal.3.25.
of the law: that is, from the neceſſitie and and c.5.13.
burden of the obſeruation of the legal ce-　Colof.2.14.
remonies: as the eating of certain meats, and 16.
the obſeruation of certaine feaſtes, and
the like. Which things in their owne na-
ture are but things indifferent, ᵇ ſo that it *b* Rom.14.
is little pertinent to godlyneſſe, ſimply
whether they be vſed, or not vſed. I ad ſimply for that in ſome reſpect, and for ſome
circűſtáce the vſe of ſuch things might be
profitable, as ſhall after appeare in place
conuenient.

VIII.

The knowledge of the doctrine of Chriſtian libertie is neceſſary alſo for the faithfull, as for peace of conſciences, ſo to auoyde ſuperſtitions.

IX.

But here notwithſtanding, obſerue, that the free vſe of externall and indifferent things, is not *granted them which as yet know not the doctrine, nor be aſſuredly perſwaded of the truth thereof: but are caried with ſome ſuperſtitious opinion, which cauſeth them to doubt of the vſe of them.

a Rom.14. v. 14, and 22.

X.

The end and vſe therefore of this doctrine is, that we may vſe the bleſſings of God, without any ſcruple of conſcience, for that end, for the which they are ordained and giuen of God for vs, but euer moderating our ſelues in the vſe of theſe things, for the 'edificatiõ of our brethren.

a Rom.14.13 15.19.20.21. & chap. 15.2 1. Cor. 10. 23.

XI.

Wherefore ſeeing the *peace of conſciences is the true and naturall end of Chriſtian libertie: it followeth that they do

a Rom. 14. 5.

do greatly abuſe the ſame, which vſe it ei-
ther to ſatisfie their owne carnall [b] luſtes,   *b* 1.Cor.6.12
or without regard of circumſtances of
time, and place, or any way[c] in contempt   *c* Rom.14.3.
of their weake brethren.   and 10.

XII.

For albeit we muſt otherwhiles [a] de-   *a* Gal.2.v.3.
fend our libertie, in the vſe of things in-   4 5.
different, before men, to repreſſe the ma-   *b* Rom.14.1.
lice of ſome froward aduerſaries, yet we   & 13.and 20
muſt haue a ſpeciall care of weake [b] bre-   and 21.
thren, that we giue no offence to them.   Act.16.3.
Rom.15.1.2.
1.Cor.8.9.&
13.& c.9. 22.

XIII.

For the right vſe of Chriſtian libertie
is, to giue place to the ignorance and infirmitie of weake brethren, and not to any
[a] Phariſaicall ſowreneſſe, or rudeneſſe of   *a* Gal.2.v.3.
hypocrites.   4.5.
Mat.1.5.14.

XIIII.

We muſt here take heed of that hypo-
criſie wherein a great nūber in this liberty, regarde not the edification of brethrē,
but prouide onely for their [a] owne peace.   *a* Gal.2.м.
& c.

XV.

And here keepe this rule. *Do not offend*
God, for thy neighbours ſake. Vnder this ge-

nerall rule are contained two ſpeciall: the
firſt is this: *looke what we are bounde to doe,*
(that is, what God hath commanded) we muſt
not leaue ² vndone for feare of any offence or
daunger that may enſue the ſame. The ſecond is this: *we muſt neither ᵇ purpoſe nor*
do any thing which God doth not permit.

XVI.

There is alſo another generall rule, *that*
loue (towardes man) *giue place to the puri-*
tie of faith: as if a man be bound to do any
thing againſt his conſcience, or elſe the
brother will be offended: let the brother
be ² offended, rather then do ᵗ any thing a-
gainſt conſcience: for as this libertie is vnder charitie, ſo charitie vnder faith.

XVII.

Againe, another conſequent of this libertie is this: *the conſciences of the faith-*
full are exempt and freed frõ the ² dominion
and power of all men: and this is, that Chriſt
may not leeſe that prayſe and thankes giuing which is due to his bountifulneſſe
and goodneſſe, and that our conſciences
may not be depriued of the fruite of his
liberalitie.

Nei-

Marginal notes:
a Mat.15.10
&c.
Iohn.6.51.
&c.
Act.5.28.29.
b Rom.3.8.
Gene.12.10.
& chap.26.7.
Exod.1.19.
Ioſ.2.4.5.6.
1.Sam.21.24.

a Luk. 14.26

a 1.Cor.3.21
& chap.7.23.

XVIII.

Neither muſt we deeme this libertie of cõſciéces in not being ſubiect vnto mã, to be but a matter of ſmall moment, for that it coſt a Chriſt ſo great a price, euen the price of his owne moſt pretious bloud.

Ibid. and 1. Pet. 1. 18. and 19. Gal. 5. 1.

XIX.

The better to vnderſtand this doctrine, we muſt note the difference betweene the ſpirituall, and ciuill gouernement of men: for by that ſpirituall regiment, the conſcience is inſtructed to ſerue and worſhip God: but by the ciuill gouernement, a man is taught to performe the duties of humanitie & ciuilitie, which muſt be obſerued and kept among men.

XX.

We muſt aduiſedly regard and ſee that theſe two regimentes be not confounded: leaſt that any infer or conclude a ciuill libertie againſt politique gouernement, by this ſpirituall libertie which Chriſt hath purchaſed for vs.

XXI.

Againe, in conſtitutions & lawes conᴄerning ſpirituall gouernement, we muſt

carefully diſcerne betweene orders lawfully and vnlawfully eſtabliſhed. For conſtitutions and orders lawfull are conſo-
nant to the word of God, but the vnlawfull are contrary to the ſame.

XXII.

Rom.13. And whereas Paule [a] commaundeth to
obey the Magiſtrate for conſcience ſake:
he doth not therein binde conſciences to
lawes politique:but this he meaneth onely, that we muſt obey the Magiſtrate ſo
far and ſo long as he commandeth things
lawful and honeſt, for that God alſo commandeth vs ſuch obedience, & we can not
with good conſcience neglect any of his
decrees. Therefore the Apoſtle doth not
here make the conſcience ſubiect to any
lawes of men, but vnto the law of God,
commanding vs to obey the lawes of men
ſo farre forth as they do not repugne the
holy lawes of God.

XXIII.

This may yet be vnderſtood,if we note
what the côſcience is. The conſcience is a
Rom.2.15. [a] feeling of Gods iudgement concerning
our actions: an eye witneſſe which diſcer-
neth

neth & can truly teſtifie of all our workes,
& this the very ſignification of the word
can teach vs.

XXIIII.

Of the premiſes we may learne , that
conſcience doth properly reſpect God, ſo
that a good conſcience is nothing els, but
the teſtimonie of our hart before God, of [a] 1.Pet.3.21
the ſinceritie of our hart.

XXV.

In deed we ſay that a good conſcience
ſometimes reſpecteth 'men, and that is in [a] Act.14.16.
reſpect of the fruites or effects thereof in
the duties of loue.

XXVI.

By the former definition of the conſcience , we may alſo learne what law bindeth the cōſciēce : namely that law which
bindeth a man ſimply without reſpect or
conſideration of men.

XXVII.

Finally the law of God, which commā-
deth in the vſe of indifferent things to regard the edification of our neighbour, al- [a] 1.Cor. 10.
though it binde the outward worke , yet 28.
bindeth it not the conſcience, [b] ſo as if a Rom. 14.22.
[b] 1.Cor.10.
28.

man might not with a good conscience
vse those things, but onely in that case of
edifying our neighbour, that is, our weake
brother.

CHAP. XV.

Of Offences.

I. APHORISME.

AN offence is a word or deed, whereby
the neighbour is offended, that is,

a Rom.14.15
Math.15.12.
Iohu.6.61. made a sad or grieued, as with any thing
impiously or vniustly spoken or done, or
when a man by any thing as well spoken,
or done (which yet is not well spoken or
b 1.Cor.8.10 done) is b moued to commit sinne.

II.

A scandale is either giuen or taken.

III.

a Math.18.6.
7.&c. That is called an offence a giuen, the
fault whereof commeth from the doer
himselfe: or an offence giuen is a wicked
word or deede, contrary to the loue of
God and our neighbour: and therfore this
euill of it selfe grieueth & maketh sad the
godly, and seduceth the weake brethren.

That

IIII.

That is called an offence ᵃ taken , when   *ᵃ Mat.15.12*
any thing not wickedly , or vntimely fpo-
ken or done , through malice or finifter
affection of minde, is wrefted to an occa-
fion of offence . Or, an offence taken is a
word or deede, of it felfe not wicked , but
taken as wicked , either malicioufly or ig-
norantly.

V.

Laftly, there feemeth alfo to be a third
ᵃ mixt offence , that is partly giuen, partly   *ᵃ Rom.14.*
taken : as when a man vfeth Chriftian li-
bertie out of feafon , not regarding time
and place conuenient . But yet this kind of
offence , is more neare & liker an offence
giuen, then taken. And this may be called
the offence of the weake ; or an offence of
infirmitie , as the other which is taken
may be called an offence Pharifaicall : for
that none thereby, but bitter fpirites, and
Pharifaicall eares are offended.   *ᵃ Rom.14.1.*
  13.21.]
VI.   *1.Cor.8.13.*

  Math.18.6.7
We muft take ᵃ heede that we offend *Math.18.6.7*
not the weake : howfoeuer proude witts *ᵇ Mat.15.14*
be ᵇ offended.   *Act 5.28.29.*
  Gal.3.4.5.

CHAP. XVI.

Of Prayer.

I. APHORISME.

a Iohn.4.24   PRayer is a ᵃholy meditation of things
            pertaining to Gods glory and our fal-
b Luke.18.1. uation: and an earneſt ᵇ deſire of the ſame,
&c.   with ſupplication, proceeding from an
c Heb.10.22 holy affiance, which(as ſonnes &ᶜ daugh-
ters)the faithfull haue in God: whereunto
alſo thankes-giuing vnto God for benefits
receiued,is vſually annexed.

II.

a Pſal.50.51.   Our preſent ⁑ neceſſitie which we feele,
b Ibid.   ought not onely to be a motiue vnto pray-
c Ibid.   er: but alſo Gods ᵇ commandement, and
Iohn.16.24. ᶜpromiſe to heare vs.
Mat.7 7.and
chap.18.19.

III.

We ought then to begge in prayer not
only for thoſe things which concerne our
owne happineſſe: but alſo that God would
a Math.4.10. giue grace that by this ſeruice and ᵃwor-
ſhip we may truly honour him.

IIII.

Againſt all diſtruſt which may hinder
                        vs

vs in prayer : we muſt oppoſe Gods holy promiſes, whereby he hath teſtified, that he will heare[a] our prayer.

a Pſal.ʃo.1ʃ.
Math.7.7.

V.

There be foure rules of prayer . The [a]firſt that we come to prayer with a mind [b]emptied of other cares , and indued with a due reuerence of the maieſtie of God, not daring to beg any thing which God himſelfe doth not permit: the ſecond, that we pray with a true ſenſe [c]and feeling of our wants , & with an earneſt deſire to obtaine : the third that in prayer we put off all[d] opinion of our own iuſtice or worthines , and contrarily, that in all humilitie, and free [e]confeſſion of our ſinnes , we flie to Gods mercy, intreating the free pardon and forgiueneſſe of our ſins : the fourth & laſt rule is , that prayer proceed from faith [f]and aſſurance of Gods grace in Chriſt: aſſuredly truſting that our prayer ſhalbe heard.

a Dan.9.3.4.
ʃ. &c.
b Mat.14.23

*c.d.e.*Luk. 18.
*v.*13.

e Dan.9.
Pſal.ʃ1.

f Rom. 10.14
Iames.1 6.
Heb.10.22.
Dan.9.17.
Pſal.ʃ1.9.

VI.

The Lord himſelfe hath giuen vs a[a] preſcript forme of prayer, which therefore is called the Lordes Prayer . This conſiſteth

a Math. 6.9.
&c.

of a Preface, narration, confirmation and conclusion.

VII.

The Preface is in these wordes, *Our Father which art in heauen.* Wherein we professe our faith, or affiance & trust we haue, as children, in God our heauenly Father, who hath by grace adopted vs in that his beloued and onely begotten Sonne our Lord Iesus Christ. Here also to lift vp our minds to God, we make mētiō of the seate of Gods maiestie, that is of heauen, where he giueth his blessed Angels the fruition of his presence, and shall giue vs in his good time appointed.

VIII.

The narration containeth sixe petitions: the first three, do in speciall manner concerne Gods glory: the other three, respect our owne benefite and good.

IX.

In the first petitiō (*Hallowed be thy name*) we are commaunded and taught to aske that, which in the third Commandement we are commanded to do : that is, that we neither thinke nor speake of God, but

with

with great reuerence : and fo in like manner of his word, and of his workes.

X.

In the fecond petition:*Let thy kingdome
come*,we beg firft,that God by the grace of
his holy fpirit, would repreffe the corrupt
affections of our nature,and forme all our
fenfes to the obedience of his will: next
that he would curbe and bridle the wicked which fight againft his kingdome,and
that he would gather vnto himfelfe his
elect , and preferue his Churches : that
he would caft downe the enemies of his
Church, and cut them fhort in all their
attempts and defires:and laftly, that in his
good time , he would make vs partakers
of his glory and heauenly bliffe.

XI.

The third petition is , *Thy will be done
in earth as it is heauen*. This petition is added to the former, for declaration fake to
helpe our ignorance :for then and there
God raigneth in the world , where men
fubmit themfelues,to be ruled by his holy
will reuealed in his word. We aske here
therefore that the holy fpirite would rule

our harts, and teach vs, that we may learne
to loue that which God loueth, & to hate
that which he hateth: that fo we may yeeld
vnto him a chearefull and willing obedience as his bleffed Angels do in heauen.

XII.

The fourth petition is, *Geue vs this day*
our dayly bread: In this petition we commende our bodies to Gods prouidence,
defiring, that he would feed, chearifh and
preferue them. And this petitiõ, the Lord
hath fet before the other two following,
(which concerne not earthly and corporall bleffings, but fpirituall and heauenly)
to helpe our dulneffe, and weakneffe, that
fo by degrees he might lift vp our mindes
to feeke after thofe greater bleffings. And
here we be willed to aske of God our
bread, that is, fuch as it fhall pleafe our
heauenly father to giue vs, for the fuften-
tation of our life: where we fee this petition is as neceffarie for the rich as for the
poore. Laftly, thefe wordes, *this day*, or
euerie day, and this Epithet *dayly* ferue to
moderate our affections and defires in
thefe tranfitorie bleffings.

The

XIII.

The fift petition, *Forgiue vs our debtes,*
as we alfo forgiue our debters: by the word
debtes he meaneth our finnes, for that we
owe the punifhment of them vnto God
and this Chrift himfelfe hath borne for
vs, in his death vpon the croffe, and fo
hath obtained the pardon of finnes for
vs . We begge that the heauenly father
would impute vnto vs that fatisfaction &
obedience of Chrift & worke in vs a fenfe
& a feeling of this imputation, that fo we
may fweetly reft in his fatherly fauour in
Chrift, and in his loue purchafed for vs
in and by the fufferings of Chrift. To this
petition is annexed an argument drawen
from the like example : that is, the example of our remiffion in pardoning our
neighbour his trefpaffes : The reafon of
which exaple doth not confift in the merite of our worke, but in the promife of
Chrift, faying. For *if ye forgiue men their* a Math.6.14.
offences, your heauenly father will alfo for- 15.
giue you. But if ye doe not forgiue men their
trefpaffes, no more will your father forgiue
you your trefpaffes. By which wordes it doth

H iij

manifeſtly appeare,that they onely can be aſſured of the pardon of ſinnes, that are aſſured and know in their conſciences, that they haue pardoned their neighbours. The reaſon whereof is this, it can not be, that any man pardon from his hart

Gods loue is cauſe of our loue, & our loue but a ſigne and effect of his loue.

his brother, vnleſſe he firſt loue him: now he can not loue his brother, which firſt doth not loue God; and no man can loue God, which is not perſwaded in his hart, that God of his meere grace hath pardoned him all his ſinnes by and through Ieſus Chriſt. And againe he that is aſſured of this, he can not, but loue God, and his neighbour in & for the Lord: from which loue, it can not be, but the pardoning of all offences muſt proceede. Laſtly this argument is alſo noted with theſe wordes

a's ij.
Forgiue vs, as we alſo forgiue.
ij ראp.

as and *alſo*,Math.6.12.and Luke.12.*For euen we, &c.* Wherefore this word *alſo* is not well omitted:for we ſay commonly, *as we forgiue them that treſpaſſe, &c.*.for, *as we alſo forgiue &c.*

XIIII.

The ſixt and laſt petition is: *And leade vs not into temptation, but deliuer vs from euill.*

euill. Where we pray for the affiftance of the holy fpirite to ouercome the temptations of the deuill, which is here called *that euill or wicked fpirite*, for that by his ὁ πονηρὸς. temptations (for which caufe he is called the tempter Math. 4. 3 .) he troubleth and vexeth vs.

XV.

And thus far of the fix petitions, contained in the narration, the confirmation followeth in thefe wordes : *For thine is the kingdome , and the power , and the glorie for ages , or for euer,* in which wordes we fhew wherefore we haue both fuch boldneffe to aske , and truft to obtaine : to wit, for that God wilbe glorified by hauing his kingdome and raigning in vs : and for that alfo he can effect what he will in heauen and earth.

XVI.

The conclufion is contained in one word, namely the word *Amen* , which is here a word of wifhing, fignifying as much as , *truth* , *So be it* , or, *Let this be a truth* . Wherefore we defire that whatfoeuer we haue prayed for at Gods hands in

the fix petitions, the fame may be true,
& effected by him. And yet there is no in-
conueniencie to fay that *Amen* here, is a
word of affeueration: for that by faith we
be affured, that God hath graunted our
requeftes.

XVII.

As for the place of prayer: God in
times paft had appointed firft his ª Taber-
nacle, then after that Salomons ᵇ Temple:
but Chrift hath ᶜ abolifhed this ceremonie of that holy place, and Paule ᵈ biddeth
vs pray in euery place. And fo Chrift ᵉ cõ-
maundeth vs to pray in our fecret cham-
bers: and himfelfe went vp to the ᶠ moun-
taine alone to pray. And Chrift alfo doth
approue a publique place of cõmon prayer, when he faith: *VVhere two or ᵍ three are
gathered together in my name, there am I
in the midft of them.*

a Exod.26.
and 40.
b 1.King.8.
2.Chron.7.
Act 8.27.
Luke.18.10.
Dan.6.10.
c Iohn.4.21.
d 1.Tim.2.8.
e Math.6.6.
f Mat.14.23.

g Mat.18.20.

XVIII.

There is no certain time in the new Te-
mẽt appointed for prayer: yet is it profitable that euery man appoint himfelf fome
ᵃ ordinarie and fpeciall houre for prayer,
as in vprifing, before and after meats, and
when

a Dan 6.10.
Pfal.55.18.
Act.10.9.

when we go to reſt, ſo that this obſeruation of ours be voyde of ſuperſtition, and
then ſpecially are we bounde to apply our
ſelues to prayer, when we ſee our ſelues,
or our brethren in any [b] dangers or in any
ſpeciall wants: againe, we are alſo bounde
to render thankes humbly vnto God, whē
we haue receiued any ſpeciall benefite at
his handes.

b Pſal.50.15
Ioel 2.
Ierem.6.26.
Eſt 4.3.&16.
c Exod.15.
Iude.5.
Pſal.9.30.34.
&c.

XIX.

Moreouer the lifting vp the voyce in
prayer, or ſinging, or geſture of the body
(as [a] kneeling, [b] couering the face, the [c] lifting vp of hands and eyes [d] towardes heauen) doe not ſimply commende any mans
prayer, but ſo far theſe things pleaſe God,
as they proceede from the true [e] affections
of the hart.

a Ephe.3.14
b 1.Cor.11.
c 1.Tim.2.8.
d Iohn.11.41
e Luke.18.11
and 13.

XX.

Againe, we muſt take heede that we
preſcribe not or appoint any certaine [a] circumſtances vnto God : for we muſt giue
him [b] leaue to graunt and performe our
requeſtes in what manner, time, and place
it pleaſeth him.

a Mat.20 21.
Iude.7.19.
b 2.Sam. 15.
26.

XXI.

Lastly, this also is to be noted, that we
[a] perseuer in prayer: and that we consider
not of the hearing of our prayers by our
sense or feeling, but by our faith. For albeit we do not alwaies feele that God doth
giue vs that we haue asked: yet we must be
assured that he doth giue & will giue, that
which is good for our saluation.

a Luke. 18.1
&c.
Luke. 11. 8.

CHAP. XVII.

Of Predestination.

I. Aphorisme.

PRedestination we call the [a] eternall decree of God, wherein he determined
with himselfe what he would haue done
with [b] euery man: as concerning their e-
ternall saluation or damnation.

a Ephe.1.4.
2.Tim.1.9.
b Rom.9.20.
21.22.& 23.

II.

This predestination hath two speciall
branches. The first is called election: the
other reprobation, by a metonymie of the
effect (that is, a change of a word properly
signifying an effect, to signifie the cause)
for election and reprobation are properly

ly referred to man : who being created, is fallen and corrupted with ſinne : but metonymically the very decree of election & reprobation is ſo [a] called.

a Ephe.1.4.

III.

Therefore we ſay with the Scripture, that God in his eternall and [a] immutable coūcell hath once decreed, whom in time to come he will [b] aduaunce to glorie : and whom on the contrarie he ſhall [c] giue ouer to condemnation.

a 2 Tim.2.
v.19.
Eſa.46.9.
Malach.3.6.
1.Theſſ.5.9.
b Rom.9.23.
c Act.1.25.
Iohn.17.12.
1.Pet.2.8.
Iude v.4.

IIII.

This purpoſe we auouch was founded on the [a] meere pleaſure of God.

a Ephe.1.5.
Rom.8.29.
Mat.11.25.
26.
Rom.9.18.

V.

Moreouer, whom God hath predeſtinate to ſaluation, them alſo hath he decreed to make partakers of the meanes by which men come to ſaluation : which meanes are their [a] recōciliation by Chriſt, their [b] effectuall calling, and [c] iuſtification. And contrarily whom he hath predeſtinate to deſtruction, them alſo hath he decreed, not to make partakers of thoſe meanes which tend to ſaluation, but to leaue [d] them to themſelues, or to deliuer

a Ephe.1.
b Rom.8.
c Ibid.

d Pſal.81.13

e Eſa.29.10.
Rom.11.8.   them to ᶜSathan that both by his and their owne naturall inſtigation they may purchaſe to themſelues damnation.

VI.

The end or ſcope of predeſtination is

a Prou.16.4.
b Ephe.1.6.
and 12.
Rom.9.23.
c Rom.9.25.
26.
d Rom.9.17
and 22.
e Rom.9.22.
f Rom.11.33
g Rom.1.18
h Rom.9.15
8.20.21.

is the glorie ᵃof God: that is, the glorie of his ᵇgrace, and mercy, manifeſted in the ſaluation of the elect, and of his ᶜiuſtice in the death of his ſonne our mediatour: the glory alſo of his ᵈpower and ᵉiuſtice in the damnation of reprobates, yea of his iuſtice, both ᶠſecret in their reiection, and alſo ᵍmanifeſt in puniſhing them, for their ſinnes: finally the glorie of his moſt free ʰpower, both in the condemnation of the reprobate, and in the glorification of his elect.

VII.

The infallible teſtimonie of our ele-

a Rom.8.30.
1.Tim.1.1.
b Rom.10.17
c Rom.8.30.
Ephe.1.7.
d 2.Tim.2.19

ction is our ᵃeffectuall calling, when as the holy ſpirite, by the preaching ᵇof the Goſpell, doth worke faith in Chriſt, in the harts of his elect, that thereby they may be ᶜiuſtified, working alſo ſome beginning of new ᵈobedience, that they may be ſanctified, that ſo in time they may be ful-

ly

ly ᵉ glorified. ᵉ Rom.8.30.

VIII.

And as the Lord ᵃ ſealeth and marketh ᵃ 2.Tim.2.19
his elect, by their vocation, iuſtification,
and ſanctification, ſo by excluding the reprobate either from the knowledge of his
truth or from the ſanctification of his ſpirite, as it were by certaine notes he ſheweth what iudgement remaineth for them.

IX.

Neither yet may any raſhly define or
pronounce, that he is in the number of
the reprobate, if the ſignes of election as
yet appeare not in him, for ſome are cal-
led, ᵃ later then others, yea the ᵇ theefe on ᵃ Math.20.3
the croſſe was not before the end of his &c.
ᵇ Luk.23.40
life called: wherefore we may deſpaire of &c.
none vnleſſe manifeſt ſignes be ſhewed,
that he hath ſinned to death: that is, a-
gainſt the holy ᶜ ſpirite, neither yet may ᶜ 1.Ioh.5.16
any ſecurely ſinne in hope of mercy, but
euer remēber *to ᵈ day, if ye heare his voyce* ᵈ Heb.3.7.
harden not your harts: for God is not mocked. ᵉ Gal 6.7.

X.

There be two notable fruits of this doctrine, the one that we may with humble

adoration , acknowledge how much we
are bounde to God, that hath vouchsafed
a Rom.11.35 to chufe vs , fo vnworthy, out of the ᵃ companie of the damned, and to aduaunce vs
to the ftate of heauenly glory . The other,
b Rom.8.31. that we may with good ᵇ affuraunce reft
&c.
2.Tim.2.19. our felues on the vnchaungeable purpofe
of God touching our faluation and therfore be fully perfwaded and affured thereof in Iefus Chrift.

CHAP. XVIII.

Of the resurrection, and of life euerlafting.

I. APHORISME.

ALbeit the doctrine of the refurrection
feeme incredible in mans reafon : yet
we that are Chriftians muft beleeue it &
receiue it : that is , we muft beleeue that
the bodies of the dead fhalbe reftored to
their firft ftate, and their foules fhall reen-
ter them againe, fo they fhall liue and rife
againe at the laft day.

II.

This faith of ours is grounded on the
tefti-

°testimonies of the word of God, who is a Dan.12.2.
almighty and can not lye. Ioh.5.29.&c

III.

But of them that shall rise againe, the
estate shalbe very vnlike. For the godly
shall rise to° life and glory euerlasting,but a Dan.12.2.
the vngodly to shame and ᵇ death euerla- b Iohn.5.29.
sting.

IIII.

This glorious and blessed resurrection
of the godly dependeth vpon the resurrection of° Christ,as of their head to whom a 1.Cor. 15.
they as members must be conformed. 12.&c.
 1.Thess.4.14

V.

Christ then the head of the godly, shal
in the resurrection make our bodies° like a Phil.5.21.
to his glorious body. 1.Cor.15.35
 &c.

VI.

Againe, Christ shall raise the dead at
his glorious° comming to iudgemēt with a 1.Thes.4.
the shout of an Archangell and sound of a 16.
trumpet.

VII.

The dead being raised, then in a mo- a 1.Thess.4.
ment as in the twinckling of an eye,the li- 16 and. 17.
uing shalbe° chaunged, so that their bo- 1.Cor.15.52
 and 53.

dies shalbe made incorruptible.

VIII.

Then streight wayes all the godly shalbe [a] caught vp into the ayre to meete the
Lord and so shall [b] euer be with the Lord
and with him enioy euerlasting happines.

a 1.Thess. 4.
17.
b Ibid.
Math.25.34.
and 46.

IX.

On the contrary, the vngodly shall together with the deuils be thrust down into [a] hell into the [b] lake that euer burneth
with fire and brimstone and there shalbe
tormented.

a Math.25.
41.and 46.
b Reue.20.15
& chap.21.8

X.

Againe, eternall life consisteth chiefly
in the full feeling of Gods loue, & in the
communion of his nature according to
these sayings, [a] *I shalbe* (saith Dauid) *satis-
fied with thine Image* : againe, [b] *in thy presence is the fulnesse of ioy and pleasures at
thy right hand for euermore* . And Peter af-
firmeth [c] that the faithfull are to this end
called that *they may be partakers of the diuine nature,* that is , of the graces of God,
his wisedome, righteousnesse, holinesse
and glory.

a Psal.17.15.
b Psal.16.18
c 2.Pet.1.4.

And

XI.

And albeit the blessed there, shall want nothing pertinent to perfect felicitie, because God shalbe [a] all in all, yet of that heauenly glory, wherewith they shalbe beautified there shalbe certaine [b] degrees as there were also [c] degrees of their giftes in this life, and as there shalbe [d] degrees of torments amongst the damed. And aboue others excelling, & most shining, shalbe the glory of the teachers of the word, that haue faithfully instructed the Church, and so brought many to righteousnesse, as [e] Daniell speaketh.

a 1.Cor. 15.
28.

b 1.Cor.15.
41.and 42.

c 1.Cor.12.4

d Mat. 10.15
and chap.11
20. &c.

[e] Dan.12.3.

XII.

This doctrine as it may iustly terrifie the vngodly; so to the godly in al miseries, and euen in death, it is [a] most comfortable, as they that know, and by the grace of God stedfastly trust, that their soule by death [b] passeth into life, and by the Angels is [c] caried into Abrahams bosome, that is, into heaué, & so to [d] Christ, & their bodies, although they rot and be eaten of wormes, yet shall in due time rise again, and be clothed with euerlasting glory.

a 1.Thess. 4.
vers. last.

b Iohn.11.25

c Luk 16.22.

d Phil. 1.23.

I

CHAP. XIX.

Of the Church.

I. APHORISME.

a Mat 26.18.
Iohn. 17. 20.
b Ephe.1 .13
Ro.10.14 15.
c Rom.8.30.
d Rom.1.7.
1.Cor.1.2.
e Ro.10.9.10.
f Rom 1.7.
1.Cor.1.2.
1.Cor.2.2.
Ephe.1.1.
g Act.2.39.
Gene.17.7.
1.Cor.7.14.

THe Church is a ᵃmultitude of men ᵇ effectually ᶜcalled by the preaching of the ᵈGospell, and therefore they be such as beleeue in Christ , and ᵉprofesse his faith, and ᶠserue God in the faith; accounting in this number with the elect, their ᵍchildren, and the children of hypocrites, which as yet by their age are not capable of this calling.

II.

The Church is either vniuersall, which commonly the Greekes call Catholicke, or particular.

III.

The vniuersall or Catholicke Church is the whole multitude of them, who from the beginning of the world, haue beleeued in Christ, that now do beleeue, and shall beleeue to the worldes end. Whereof one part now triumpheth in heauen, to wit, the faithfull that are departed:

another part is militant on the earth, that
is, the faithfull, that yet liue. And this a-
gain, is diuided into particular Churches.

IIII.

A Particular Church is a particular
Congregation of the faithfull, dwelling
together in one place, & exercifing them *a* 1.Cor.1 2,
felues in Gods worfhip according to the 2.Cor.1.1.
direction of his word. Gal.1.2,
1.Theff.1.1;
2.Theff.1.1.

V.

A Particular Church may be diftingui-
fned in the old and the new.

VI.

By the old I meane that which was before Chriftes incarnation, as the Church
of the Iewes, which then did excel as touching the forme of outward gouernmēt.

VII.

I call that the new Church, which began after Chrifts comming, efpecially after his afcenfion in heauen, being gathe-
red out of diuerfe nations: and this is cal- *a* Ephe.2.13,
led *b* the Chriftian Church. *b* Act.11.26.

VIII.

Where the Church is diftinguifhed *a* Rom.2.28,
in the inuifible and vifible, it may not be 29. &c.11.7.

I ij

thought that there be two Churches of diuerſe kinds, but one & the ſame Church in diuerſe reſpectes may be ſaid to be viſible and inuiſible.

IX.

And it is called inuiſible for that it can not be ſeene with mens eies: for that faith, by which the Church hath her being in *a* Rom.2.29. Chriſt, is placed in the [a] hart, which none *b* Act.1.24. but [b] God can ſee.

X.

But it is ſaid to be viſible, for that it hath certain markes, which may be ſeene, and whereby we may conclude aſſuredly that there is a Church & people of God: *a* 1.Ioh.2.19. albeit [a] hypocrites be mingled with them, Math.13.3. &d. Item 43. who profeſſe the ſame faith, & yet beleeue &c. not in Ieſus Chriſt. *a* Ephe.2.20. Act.2.24.

XI.

b 1.Cor.1.13. Theſe markes are the [a] pure preaching 1.Cor.12.20. of the word, and lawfull adminiſtration of and 23. Mat.laſt v.19 the [b] Sacraments. and 20. Mar.laſt.v. 15.and 16.

XII.

a Mat.18.15. For albeit in the Church of God, holy 16.17. [a] diſcipline be alſo required: yet if here the 1.Cor.5.5. gouernours of the Churches be ſlacke in their

their duties, the Church is not prefently 👉
to be thought no Church, as long as the
two former markes remaine.

XIII.

And yet further I ad ,there may creep
in fome corruption,both in ᵃ doctrine and $\quad$ *a* Cor.3. 12.
in the adminiftratiõ of the ᵇSacraments:& $\quad$ *b* 1.Cor. 11.
yet it fhall not ceafe to be a Church, as $\quad$ 12.
long as the ᶜ foundation is retained,which $\quad$ *c* 1.Cor.3.11.
is Chrift, or faluation by Chrift alone.

XIIII.

It is the dutie of euery godly man, to
ᵃ ioyne himfelf to fuch a congregation, or $\quad$ *a* Heb.10.25
focietie, as he feeth to haue thofe markes $\quad$ 1.Cor.11.20
and (as ᵇ much as lyeth in him) to profeffe $\quad$ *b* Pfal.48.
himfelfe a member thereof, and to keepe
in holy communion & felowfhip with it.

XV.

It is called the holy Church, partly be-
caufe it is wafhed &ᵃ purged by the bloud $\quad$ *a* 1.Iohn.1.7
of Chrift: partly becaufe it is fanctified by $\quad$ Eph.5.25.26
his ᵇ holy fpirit and by Gods grace hath a $\quad$ *b* Rom.8.1.
ᶜ growth in fanctificatiõ, vntill at length it $\quad$ Eph.5.26.27
be fully perfected,which fhalbe when this $\quad$ Pfal.15.
life is ᵈ ended. $\quad$ *c* Ephe.4.13.
$\qquad$ *d* Phil.3. 12.
$\qquad$ & chap.1.6.

I iij

CHAP. XX.

Of the Ministers of the Church.

I. Aphorisme.

ALbeit God alone inlighteneth and ruleth the harts of his elect: yet becauſe
it pleaſeth him herein to vſe the ᵃ Mini-
ſterie of men it is our partes with ᵇ reuerence to embrace thoſe things, which by
his ſeruaunts he teacheth vs for our good
inſtruction and comfort.

a 1.Cor.3 5.
2.Cor.5.20.
b 1.Cor.4.1.
Gal.4.15.

II.

The ſeruants of God or Miniſters, are
ſome continuing and as ordinarie, ſome
but for a time and as extraordinarie.

III.

In the old Teſtament the continuing
and ordinarie Miniſters of the Church
were Patriarches, Prieſts and Leuites: the
temporall & extraordinarie the Prophets.

IIII.

In the new Teſtament, the perpetuall
and ordinarie are ᵃPaſtours & ᵇTeachers:
the temporall and extraordinary were the
Apoſtles, ᵈProphets and ᵉEuangeliſtes.

a.b.c.d.e.
Ephe.4.11.

God

V.

God reuealed himſelfe to the Patriarches, as [a]Adam, [b]Noah, [c]Abraham, [d]I-
ſaac, [e]Iacob, [f]Ioſeph, by apparitions, vi-
ſions, and dreames, and ſo gouerned their
families.

a Gene.3.
b Ge. 6.7.8.9
c Gen.12.13.
15.17.18.21.
22.
d Gen.25.11
& 22.& c.26.
2.3.4.5.
e Gen.28.31.
32.35.
f Gene. 37.

VI.

He preſcribed certain lawes by Moſes,
for the Prieſtes and [a]Leuites, that ſo they
might by them gouerne the Church of Iſraell.

a In Leuit.

VII.

But as for the Prophets he raiſed them
vp [a]extraordinarily, to [b]inſtruct and to [c]ex-
cite the people, and the Prieſtes, if they er-
red or were negligēt in their duties : theſe
did alſo foreſhewe what [d] puniſhmentes
ſhould fall vpon Gods people for their
negligence, and what [e]euils ſhould come
vpon their enemies for their deſtruction:
but principally they comforted the faithful with Prophecies of Chriſts comming:
and therfore they preach often of his [f]con-
ception, [g]natiuitie, [h]paſſion, death, reſurrection, and euerlaſting kingdome.

a Eſ. 6.
Ierem.1.
Ezech.2.&c.
b Eſa.1. &c.
c Eſa. 2.
d Eſa.3.29.
&c.
e Eſa.13 . &c.

f Eſa.7.14.
g Eſa.9.6.
Mich 5.2.
h Eſa. 53.
i Eſa.11.59.
61.&c.

I iiij

VIII.

And thus farre of the Ministers of the old Testament : now touching the Ministers of the new Testament. The Lord in the beginning of his kingdome raised vp [a] Apostles, [b] Prophets, [c] Euangelistes, and whē the Churches were founded & planted by them, he ordained that Pastors and [d] Teachers should succeede and continue for euer.

[a] Mat.28.19
[b] Act.11.27.
[c] Act.8.5.&c
[d] Ephe.4.11

IX.

The Apostles were [a] immediatly called of Christ, and sent into the whole [b] world, that so they might set vp the kingdome of God in all places.

[a] Mat.4.18.
&c.
Ioh.1.37.&c.
Act 9.& 22.
[b] Mar.16.15
Act.9.15.
Rom.15.15.
20.

X.

He raised vp also at this time Prophets, who had speciall [a] reuelation and gifts for the interpretation of holy Scriptures : and these did sometimes foreshew by the spirite, any matter of waight which should come, either on the [b] Church, or to any [c] one of the faithfull.

[a] 1.Cor.14.
29 &c.

[b] Act.11.28.
[c] Act.21.10.

XI.

Againe, the Apostles had the Euangelistes for their [a] companions, whom they tooke

[a] Act.16.1.

tooke with them to fupplie their abfence
in preaching of the Gofpell, and in ᵇ efta- ᵇ Tit.1.5.
blifhing the Churches : and fuch were ᶜ2.Tim.4.11.
ᶜLuke, ᵈTimothie and ᵉTitus. ᵈ2.Tim 4.5.
ᵉ2.Cor.8.23

XII.

Then folowed Paftours, and Teachers
which the Church can neuer want.

XIII.

And thus farre of Churches offices,
which did confift in the Minifterie of the
word : There be two other ordinarie alfo, which ought to remaine euer in this
ᵃChurch:Church-gouernement, and the ᵃ Rom.12.8
care of the poore.

XIIII.

Church ᵃ Gouernours are chofen men ᵃ1.Cor.12.
fet ouer the people, for ᵇ correction of ᵇ1.Cor.5. 28.
manners, affiftantes with the Bifhops and 2.Cor.1.6.7.8
Paftours.

XV.

The care of the poore, partly belon-
geth to the Deacons ᵃor Collectors that ᵃ Act.6.3.
diftribute the almes, partly to them which 1.Tim.3.8.
vifite the fick, & fuch in Paules time were &c.
certaine ᵇauncient and honeft widowes. ᵇ 1.Tim.5.9.

XVI.

And thus farre of the duties of Church officers, now as touching their calling these foure points are to be obserued: first what kinde of persons are to be called, secondly how, thirdly by whom, lastly with what rite or ceremonie they must be ordained.

XVII.

As concerning the first, I say that Bishops and Pastours, and Teachers, are to be chosen that are of sound [a] doctrine, and [b] holy life, fit and [c] able to teach. The [d] gouernors also must be furnished with good giftes, wisedome, and iudgement, to discharge their duties.

*a.b.c.*1.Tim.3
2.&c.
Tit.1.6. &c.
d 1.Tim.3. 8.
&c.

XVIII.

Secondly, in this election & ordinance of the Ministers of Christ, men must proceede in a religious feare, and testifie the same before, by [a] fasting and prayer.

a Act.15. 23.
Act.13.2.3.

XIX.

Thirdly, they must be men approued and knowen of the [a] gouernors for knowledge and learning, & which haue a good name in the Church amõg the faithful for
life

a Act.1.15.
&c.
Act.6.2.&c.

life and conuerſation.

XX.

Fourthly, they were ordained in times paſt by the Apoſtles and their ſucceſſors, with[a] impoſition or laying on of handes: which rite for comelineſſe and order ſake may well be obſerued in theſe dayes , ſo that we put no opinion of neceſſitie or of worſhip therein.

[a] Act.13.3.
1.Tim.4. 14.
2.Tim.1.6.
1.Tim.5.22.

CHAP. XXI.

Of Church diſcipline and gouernement.

I. APHORISME.

ECcleſiaſticall céſure or Church diſcipline is a[a] brotherly [b] correction according to Gods word, wherby the faithfull are ſtirred vp to do their duties, and ſo they further the ſaluation one of another.

[a] 2.Tim.3.16
Mat.18.15.
2.Cor.2.6.
2.Theſſ.3.15
[b] Mat.18.15
1.Cor.5.11.
2.Theſſ.3.15

II.

This diſcipline is either common or proper : common, whereunto all ought to be ſubiect : proper , which pertaineth to the Miniſters of the Church onely.

III.

The common diſcipline doth reſpect, three degrees in priuate or ſecret ſinnes. The firſt is, that he that hath ſinned be admoniſhed, and reproued priuatly of him, to whom alone that ſinne was knowen: the ſecond, that if he deſpiſe his correction, then he muſt be rebuked and admoniſhed before one or two witneſſes: the third that if he contemne their admonition alſo, he muſt be admoniſhed by the Church, that is, the gouernours and iudges, which are appointed by the Church.

*Mat.18.15
16.17.*

*1.Tim.4.14
1.Tim 5.17.
1.Cor.12.28.
Rom.12.8.*

IIII.

But if ſinnes be open and manifeſt, then there is no need to proceede by thoſe degrees: for the gouernors muſt not delay to proceede in the cenſure and correction of ſuch ſinners.

*1.Tim.5 20
1.Cor.5.*

V.

For the correction of light ſinnes reproofe onely may ſuffice, but grieuous ſinnes and great offences and contempt or contumacie againſt the cenſures and admonitions eccleſiaſticall, muſt be puniſhed with excommunication.

*Mat.18.15
1.Tim 5 20.
1.Cor.5.5.
and 13
Mat.18.17.*

Excom-

VI.

Excommunication is the [a] iudgement or decree of the [b] Church, whereby any [c] member of the same Church, for offending the Church by some [d] grieuous sinne, or great [e] contempt, is giuen ouer to [f] Sathan, (according to the charge of [g] Christ) that is, he is effectually [h] declared to be vnder the power and dominion of the deuill, and to haue no right or interest in the kingdome of the Church of Christ: and therefore this man is kept also from the communion of the Lordes Supper, vntill [k] he giue a probable signification & testimonie of his repentance.

[a] 1.Cor.5.4.
[b] 2.Cor.2.6.
[c] 1.Cor.5.11
[d] Ibid.1. & 11
[e] Mat.18.17.
[f] Ibid.1.Cor. 5.4.
[g] Ibid.5.
[h] Ibid.4.
Math.18.18.
Iohn.20.23.

[i] Mat.18.17
1.Cor.5.11.
and 13.
[k] 2.Cor.2.6.
7.8.

VII.

But yet these religious and wise gouernors must temper the seueritie of excommunication with the spirite of [a] meekenesse, *least* [b] *this man be swallowed vp with ouer much heauinesse.*

[a] Gal.6.1.
[b] 2 Cor.2.7.

VIII.

The ende which the Church in these censures and excommunications, principally respecteth are three. The first, that they which liue an vncleane and wicked

life, ſhould not be numbred among Chriſtians, to the diſhonour and ª prophana-
tion of the name of God. The ſecond, leaſt
the godly ſhould be ᵇ corrupted by the
continuall conuerſation of the wicked.
The third, that the excommunicate being
confounded and ªſhamed may ſo ᵈ repent
and be ſaued.

a 1.Cor.5.1.
Rom.2.24.
b 1.Cor.5.6.

c 2.The.3.14
d 1.Cor.5.5.

IX.

a 2.The.3.14
2.Cor.5 9.11

We muſt not conuerſe ª with an excō-
municate perſon but in priuate and do-
meſticall duties, leaſt we cheariſh and increaſe his cōtempt by any familiaritie: but
ſo ſoone as he giueth any probable teſtimonie of his repentance, he muſt be receiued into our ſocietie and communion
ᵇ of the Church againe.

b 2.Cor.2.6.
&c.

X.

And thus farre of the common diſcipline: The diſcipline proper to the Miniſters of the Church, is contained in certaine Canons, which the auncient Bi-
ſhops did preſcribe for themſelues and
their order: of which ſorte are theſe. *That
no Clergie man or Miniſter, be a hunter,
dicer, reueller, or pot-companion. Item, that*

no Minifter practife vfurie, or any mar-
chandife : that none be prefent at wanton la-
fciuious dances, and the like, &c.

CHAP. XXII.

Of Vowes.

I. APHORISME.

A Vow is an holy promife made to God.
II.

A vow is either generall or fpeciall.
III.

A generall vow, is that which Chriftiãs
make in their Baptifme, where renouncing Sathã, they giue themfelues to God
to ferue him, that they may obey his ho- *a Mar.28.19*
ly Commaundements, and notfulfill the
wicked luftes of the flefh.
IIII.

A fpeciall or particular vowe, is that
which any man moued with fome [a] fpeci- *a Gen.28.20*
all reafon maketh vnto God. *&c. Iud.1.30.*
1.Sam.1.11.
V. *2.Sam.15.8.*

In a lawfull fpeciall vow, foure things *Act.18.18.*
Num.16.
are required: of which the firft is, that
we be [a] affured that our vowe be [b] agree- *a Rom.14.23*
b Act.23.12.

e 2.Cor.7.7. able to Gods word; the second, that it be
d 1.Cor.7.4. not aboue the ftrength which God hath
giuen vs; the third, that it be agreeable to
our vocation; the fourth, that we vow with
a good purpofe of hart, and for a lawfull
end.

VI.

The right and lawfull endes of vowes
be foure, of which the two former are in
refpect of the time paft: the other two in
refpect of time to come.

VII.

The firft end of a lawfull vow, is to te-
a Gen.28.20 ftifie a thankefulneffe to God for benefites receiued.

VIII.

The fecond end of a lawfull vow, is to
chaftife and afflict our felues for fome fins
cōmitted, that we may be the more fit to
a 1.Cor. 11. entreate God to remoue his wrath frō vs.
31.

IX.

The third end is, to make vs the more
a 1.Cor.6.12 warie and heedfull againft finne, by de-
1.Cor.9. 27. priuing our felues of the vfe for a time of
fome fpeciall things.

The

X.

The fourth end is to ftirre vp our felues
as it were with a fpurre to our dutie, binding our felues thereunto by a vow.

XI.

That the Monafticall vowes, are vnlawfull & vngodly, it is manifeft by foure reafons. Firft, becaufe the life Monafticall is
imagined a worfhip of God: fecondly, be- *a* Math. 15.9
caufe they vow a Monafticall life, without
refpect of Gods calling, and without approbation from him: thirdly, becaufe the
Monkes and Nunnes, bind themfelues to
many vile and vngodly feruices : fourthly,
becaufe they promife to God perpetuall
virginitie, when as yet, either they haue
not the gift of continencie, or if they haue *b* Mat.19.11.
it, be vncertaine how long to haue it. 1.Cor.7.7.

XII.

Vowes are of this ftrength and nature,
that if they be lawfull they *a* bind, but if *a* Deut 23.21
they be *b* vnlawfull they are voyde and of *b* Iud.11.
none effect. Act.23.21.

K

CHAP. XXIII.

Of the Sacraments.

I. Aphorisme.

a Exo.12. 26
b Deut.12.32
1.Cor.11.23
c Gen.17.10.
d Gen.17.11.
Rom.4.11.
e Gene.17.7.
Ier.31.33.34
a Heb.9.15.
b Gal.3.1.

SAcraments are ᵃceremonies ordained ᵇof God to illuſtrate and to ſeale vnto his ᶜpeople the ᵈpromiſe of grace, contained in Gods holy ᵉcouenant.

II.

Sacraments do ᵃilluſtrate the promiſe of grace, as liuely ᵇpictures, in that they repreſent and typically ſet before the beleeuers, the ſacrifice of Chriſt and the efficacie thereof.

III.

a Pſal.81.6.
Rom.4.1.

b Mat.26.28.

But they ſeale, in that they be diuine ᵃteſtimonies ordained to teſtifie the ſame thing, which the promiſe it ſelfe doth teſtifie, to wit, that Chriſt by his ᵇſacrifice hath purchaſed for the beleeuers forgiueneſſe of ſins, the grace of the holy ſpirite, and life euerlaſting.

IIII.

Againe, the holy Ghoſt by the Sacraments illuſtrating the promiſe of grace doth

doth inſtruct the faithfull in the myſterie
of ſaluation, and by ſealing it perſwades
the truth of the promiſe and ſo confirmes
faith.

V.

Yet they do performe neither of both
themſelues by any vertue in them, but in
that the holy ᵃſpirit worketh by them, and
his working is free, ᵇ ſo that he worketh
where he will, when he will, and in what
meaſure it pleaſeth him.

ᵃ Ephe.1. 13
14.& chap.4.
v. 30.
ᵇ Iohn.3.8.

VI.

The Sacramentes, ſome are of the old
Teſtament, ſome of the new.

VII.

The Sacraments of the old Teſtament
were ᵃCircumciſion, ᵇpurifications, and
ᶜſacrifices, & of theſe the ᵈpaſſeouer was
a ſpeciall Sacrament.

ᵃ Gene.17.
Leuit.12.
ᵇ Leuit.14.
ᶜ Leu.1,3,4.
6.&c.
ᵈ Exod.12.
2.Paral.35.

VIII.

Circuciſio did illuſtrate the promiſe of
grace vnder the type of cutting off, of the
foreskin of the fleſh: for by the circumci-
ſing of the foreskin was ſignified, that the
ſins of the faithful were done away by for-
giuenes of ſins, or free ᵃiuſtification. Cir-

ᵃ Rom.4. 11.

cumcifion did alfo feale the promife of grace, by applying the fame to euery perfon, fo that the couenant of God was as it were fealed in euery mans flefh.

c Gen.17.13.

IX.

The purifications did illuftrate the promife of grace, vnder the type of wafhing, for by them was fignified that the finnes of the faithfull, were purged by the bloud of Chrift and dayly are wafhed away by the holy Ghoft.

a Leu.14.7.8

X.

The facrifices did illuftrate the promife of grace, as being types of our expiatorie facrifice, for by them was fignified that Chrift fhould be flaine for an expiatorie facrifice, that is, to fatisfie for all the finnes, of all the elect.

a Leuit.1.4. & 4.20.& 16. 27.30.
b Heb.9.26. & 28.& c.10. 11.12.14.

XII.

The pafcall lambe not onely fhadowed this as a facrifice generally, but alfo forefhewed fome peculiar thing of Chriftes facrifice, to wit, that his bones fhould not be broken, and it fignified that the foules of the faithfull did banquet and feed vpõ Chrift, as it were fpiritually, in a facrifice,

a Iohn.19.36

b 1.Cor.5.7. and 8.

that

that is , they receiued hereby some feeling of Gods grace & loue , purchased for
them, by the sacrifice of Christ. Againe, it
represented the holinesse of Christes sacrifice, for it was commanded to be an vn-
spotted' abe.

ᶜ Exod. 12.5.

XII.

But' ides this shadowing of Christes
sacrifice respect whereof that ceremonie of eating the lambe was a Sacrament,
it was also ordained to prayse God , for
deliuerance out of the bondage of Egipt.

ᵃ Exo.12.27.

XIII.

And thus much of the Sacraments of
the old Testament. The Sacramentes of
the new are two, Baptisme and the Lords
Supper.

XIIII.

Baptisme, that succeeded in place of
Circumcision, doth illustrate the promise
of grace , vnder the type of washing , for
as by water the filthinesse of the body is
done away ; so by the bloud of Christ
shed on the Crosse, and by faith sprinckled
on our harts , our soules are purged from
sinne. But Baptisme sealeth vnto vs the

ᵃ Col.2.11.
12.

ᵇ Act.22.16.

ᶜ 1.Pet.3.21.

ᵈ 1.Iohn.1.7

promiſe of grace, in that euery one is waſhed in that water, which is the Sacramēt
of the bloud of Chriſt ſhed on the croſſe.

XV.

The Supper of the Lord, which came
a Luk.22.15. &c. ᵃ in place of the paſſeouer, doth illuſtrate
the promiſe of grace, partly by repreſen-
b Luk.22. 19.
1.Cor.11.24. ting the paſſionᵇ of Chriſt, by the breaking
ofthe bread, & by pouring forth the wine,
c Luk.22. 20. the ᶜ ſhedding ofhis bloud : and partly by
declaring the efficacie of Chriſtes death,
d 1.Cor. 5.8. by this ioyfull ᵈ bāquet, for that the ſoules
of the faithfull ſweetely banquet, & be cō-
forted in taſting of Gods fauour & grace
purchaſed by the death of Chriſt . But
it ſealeth vnto vs the promiſe of grace,
in that the bread which is giuen to euery
one of vs to be eaten , is the Sacrament of
Chriſtes body crucified for vs, and in that
euery one of vs , doth drinke ofthe cup,
which is the Sacrament of the bloud of
Chriſt ſhed vpon the croſſe for vs.

XVI.

And the Supper of the Lord, hath the
nature not onely of a Sacrament, but alſo
of a ſacrifice, to wit, of thankes-giuing, as
alſo

alſo the lambe, which had this place before it. For as that lambe was appointed
to prayſe God for their deliuerie from the
bōdage of Pharao,ſo the holy Supper was
ordained to ªprayſe the Lord for our re-   *a* 1.Cor.11.
demption from the power of the deuill by   26.
the death of Chriſt.

XVII.

But as the Sacramentes in reſpeċt of
God, are ſignes of grace towards his peo-
ple; ſo in reſpeċt ofvs they be ªmarkes of   *a* Mat.23.15
our profeſſion, whereby we openly pro-   Aċt.2.41.&
feſſe that we deſire to be counted among   chap. 8.36.
the people of God, and will worſhip one-   37.38.
ly the true God,who hath manifeſted him
ſelfto his people,as by the moſt ſure word   *a* Gen.17.10
and doċtrine of the Prophetes and Apo-   and 11.
ſtles, ſo alſo by theſe Sacraments.   Exod.12. 11.
                                             and 27.
XVIII.   Aċt.22. 16.
                                             Mat.26. 26.
Of all theſe Sacraments, the Scripture   and 28.
vſually ſpeaketh ªmetonymically,that is,   Mar.14. 22.
attributing the names or properties of   and 24.
the things ſignified to the ſignes them-   Luke.22. 19.
ſelues, which thing is done, partly to   and 20.
teach vs ,the relation which is betweene   1.Cor.10.4.
thoſe ſignes,and things ſignified, & part-   16.
                                             1.Cor.11.24
            K iiij   and 25,

ly to fignifie the truth & certaintie of the
working of thofe holy Sacramentes, that
the beleeuers fhould not doubt, but that
the things fignified, fet before vs, are as
truly by the working of the holy fpirit cō-
municated vnto them, as they certainly
feele, that thefe diuine fignes and feales
(which are named Sacraments) are by the
Minifter of the Church giuen them.

XIX.

The difference of the old and new Sacramēts, is not in the things fignified, for
they, in both are the fame, but partly in
the manner of fignification, and partly in
the euidence of demonftration, for the old
fignified and figured Chrift to come, but
the new fignifie and fhew that he is come.
Again, the new are more manifeft thē the
old, becaufe they reprefent a thing done,
and clearely preached by the Gofpell.

a 1.Cor.10,
2.3 4.

XX.

They erre that any way bind the things
fignified to the fignes,

XXI.

As alfo they that attribute to the fignes
power to conferre grace, which they onely

ly feale and teftifie.

XXII.

But the Papiftes erre moſt ſhamefully, in that they transforme the Lords Supper into the Maſſe, teaching that by confecration, that is, by the muttering of the fiue wordes, *Hoc enim eſt corpus meum*, *for this is my body* ouer the bread, the fame is tranſubſtantiated into, or turned into the ſubſtance of the body of Chriſt, as they ſay: and by the offring vp of Chriſt thus created by the Prieſt, all their ſins, for whom the Maſſe is celebrated, are purged, whether they be as yet aliue, or euē long ſince dead, and in Purgatorie.

XXIII.

Laſtly they ſinne alſo grieuouſly whiles they adore that fained Chriſt, as lying hid vnder the forme of bread.

CHAP. XXIIII.

Of Baptifme.

I. Aphorisme.

Baptiſme is the firſt Sacrament of the new Teſtament, or couenant of grace,

◄ Mat. 28. 19 wherein according to Chrifts inftitution the Chriftian is dipped in water or fprinkled with water , by the Minifter of the Church, to reprefent the fhedding of the bloud of Chrift vpon the Croffe , and to teftifie to him, that the remiffion of finsis purchafed for him by the bloud of Chrift, and to feale his regeneration by the holy Ghoft , which grace is purchafed alfo fot the elect, by the bloud of Iefus Chrift: and laftly to feale his communion and felowfhip with Chrift in the kingdome of heauen : and fo in like manner the Baptifed makes publique profeffion , that his harts defire is to be one of the people and Church of God.

I I.

Whereas we fay that Baptifme is a Sacrament, we haue already fhewed in the former Chapter what this word fignifieth.

I I I.

We ad that Baptifme is a Sacrament of the new Teftament , or couenant of grace, becaufe it was inftituted by Chrift after his incarnation : firft adminiftred amongft the Iewes by Iohn the Baptift, &
Chrift

Chriſt himſelfe, next among all nations
by the Apoſtles and their ſucceſſours.

IIII.

We call Baptiſme the firſt Sacrament
of the new Teſtament, in reſpect of the ſecond, which is the Lords Supper: for Bap-
tiſme is the Sacrament of our firſt ᵃ en- **ᵃ Act.2.4.1.**
trance, and admiſſion into the viſible **Iohn.4 1.**
Church of Chriſt, that we may be of the
number of Gods childrẽ & ſo accounted,
& may enioy their ᵇpriũiledges. And ther- **ᵇ Ibid.v.42.**
fore men vnbaptiſed may not be admit-
ted to the Lordes Supper, like as in times
paſt vnder the old Teſtament, the Sacra-
crament of their firſt ᶜ entrance into the **ᶜ Mat.23.15.**
Church was Circumciſion, and none ᵈ vn- **ᵈ Exod.13.48**
circumciſed was to eate the paſſeouer.

V.

We ſay that the perſon to be Baptiſed
ought to be a ᵃ Chriſtian : by which name **ᵃ Mar.16.16**
we vnderſtand not onely men of yeares, **Act.8.36.37.**
lately conuerted to the Chriſtiã faith, but **38.**
Act.2.41.
alſo young ᵇ infants the children of Chri- **Act.16.14.**
ſtian parents : whereby may appeare that **15.31.32.33.**
ᵇ Act.16. 33.
the ſpeach of the common people is erro- **Exod.12.48.**
neous, when as deſiring Baptiſme of the

Paftour of the Church for their infants,
they fay, *God hath giuen me a child, I pray
you make it a Chriftian foule*. For Baptifme
doth not make a Chriftian, but fignifieth
and marketh vs for Chriftians.

VI.

Vve adde further that Baptifme is to
be adminiftred by the Minifter of the
Church: bicaufe Baptifme is a part of the
Ecclefiafticall [a] Minifterie, which none
may [b] meddle with but they which are
thereunto lawfully called : for to whom
Chrift gaue cõmiffion to Baptife, to them
alfo he gaue charge to preach his holy
word: and what God hath ioyned together, [c] no man may put afunder. Thofe
women therfore finne, which in their fained caufe of neceffitie do adminifter this
holy Sacrament: yea they fin dangeroufly,
for baptizing without any commiffion frõ
God, nay [d] contrary to his word: and for a-
fcribing to any externall thing our euerlafting faluation, which is to be fought
only in the death of Chrift and in the promife of grace. The fame is to be thought
alfo if any man not called to the Miniftery
of

[a] Mat.28.19
[b] Heb.5.4.

[c] Mat.19.6.

[d] 1.Cor.14.
34.
1.Tim.2.22.

of the Goſpell do Baptiſe.

VII.

Water onely is to be vſed in Baptiſme and no other liquor: for that Gods commandement is of water only, and the practiſe of the faithfull ſeruauntes of God, which firſt miniſtred the ſame (as Iohn Baptiſt, Chriſt and his Apoſtles and their ſucceſſours) can teach vs.

VIII.

And whether the Baptized be dipped in water, and that once or thriſe, or haue the water ſprinkled or powred vpon him, it is a matter indifferent, and ought to be free in the Church according to the diuerſitie of countreys. For although it be manifeſt that dipping in the water was vſed in the *ᵃ* primitiue Church: yet the originall Baptizing doth ſignifie not onely to be dipped in the water, but alſo to be wet with water any way.

ᵃ Iohn.3.23.
Mat.3.16.
Act.8.38.39.
Rom.6.4.5.
βαπλίζοϳ.

IX.

Moreouer Baptiſme is giuen vs of God to this end: firſt for the confirmation of our owne faith to our ſelues, next for the manifeſtatiō of our profeſſion among mē.

Baptiſme

X.

Baptiſme helpes our faith three wayes, teſtifying vnto vs of three things, which we receiue by faith: for firſt it is an inſtruction and ſymbole thereunto, of the ᵃ remiſſion of ſinnes, next of our ᵇ renouation by the holy Ghoſt, laſtly of our vnion and ᶜ communion with Chriſt.

a Act.2.37.
& c.22.16.
b Rom.6.4.
Tit.3.5.
c Gal.3.28.

XI.

Firſt concerning forgiueneſſe of ſins, Baptiſme both teacheth and ſealeth the ſame in a ſpeciall manner vnder the figure and type of waſhing ᵃ & purging vs : for as by water the filthines of the body is purged and waſhed away, So by the bloud ᵇ of Chriſt all the pollutions of the faithfull are waſhed and purged.

a 'Act.22.16
Soph.5.26.
Tit.3.5.6.
b Iohn.1.7.

XII.

And this confirmation which we haue by Baptiſme concernes the whole life, all, and euery one of the ſinnes of our life: for the bloud of Chriſt, whereof Baptiſme is the ſeale, purgeth ᵃ vs from all ſinne. Therfore ſo ofté as we fall, we ſhould call our Baptiſme to minde, and thereby arme our ſelues, that we may euer reſt aſſured
of

a 1.Iohn.1.7

of the free pardon of our finnes, for that
the bloud of Chrift is that fotūaine which
is ᵇ opened to the houfe of Dauid and to ᵇ Zach. 13.1.
the inhabitants of Ierufalem, that is, to all
the faithfull, to wafh them from fin, and
from vncleaneffe.

XIII.

Let no mā by this doƈtrine gather any
libertie to finne : for this doƈtrine is not
taught, but for the confolation of them
which be truly humbled, and for afflicted
foules and confciences. Againe, Baptifme
doth no leffe warne vs of our ª mortifica- ª Rom. 6.4.
tion and dying vnto finne, then of the remiffion of our finnes by Chrift.

XIIII.

Therefore the fecond end of our Bap-
tifme is our ª regeneration: for this Chrift ª Tit 3.5.
promifeth to worke in vs by his holy fpi-
rite, and fo doth indeede : and this grace
alfo he merited for vs of his father, by his
death and paffion.

XV.

Where we muft obferue that this re-
newing of nature is ª imperfect in this life: ª Rom. 7.
but yet fo be we renewed that this finne

b Rom.6.4. dwelling in vs, raigneth b not, nor hath dominion ouer vs: but by the grace of Gods
spirite is dayly more and more mortified
in vs.

XVI.

The third benefite by Baptisme, is our
holy vnion and communion with Christ:
a 1.Cor.11. that we may know, that we are vnited a and
15.   receiued to felowship with Christ & knit
vnto him as the members to the head: and
therfore shalbe coheires with him in heauen. For Christ to this end sanctified Bap-
b Math.3.16. tisme in b his owne body, that he might
haue it as commō with vs, that so it might
be as a most sure bande of our vnion and
communion with him. And Paule hereby
proueth vs to be the sons of God, because
c Gal.3.14. that in Baptisme we haue put c on Christ;
that is, because by the seale and testimony
of our Baptisme, were are ioyned vnto
Christ the onely begotten sonne of God.

XVII.

And thus these three ends of Baptisme
serue right well for the confirmation of
our faith, and so may minister great comfort vnto vs. Againe, for our profession,
among

among men, Baptiſme is a badge of that,
for thereby we teſtifie that our deſire is,
to be numbred among Gods people, pro-
feſſing that we conſent with all Chriſtiãs
in one forme of the religious worſhip of
one God onely, and this profeſſion alſo
reſpecteth the glory of God. And this
meaning hath Chriſt, when he commandeth to baptize *in the name of the Father,
the Sonne and the holy Ghoſt*: that is, that by
Baptiſme men may be bounde to worſhip
the true God, who is Father, Sonne and
holy Ghoſt: and that this phraſe is ſo to be
vnderſtood, the very wordes of the Apoſtle can teach vs. 1. Cor. 1. v. 12. 13. 14. 15.

a Iohn. 4. 1.
Act. 2. 41.

b Mat. 28. 19.
εἰς τὸ ὄνομα.

XVIII.

Now by the premiſſes learne, that they
onely rightly receiue and rightly vſe Baptiſme, which referre it to the ends for the
which Chriſt ordained it, that is, that they
may feele, and by faith receiue remiſſion
of ſins, regeneration and life euerlaſting
in Chriſt alone: & ſo receiue Baptiſme as
Gods holy ſeale of all theſe benefites.

XIX.

Therfore thoſe men greatly abuſe Bap-

L

tifme , which feeke remiffion of finnes in that externall actiō:as if the power of wafhing away finnes were fhut vp in the very element , or at the leaft in the bloud of Chrift as lying hid therein.

CHAP. XXV.

The Baptisme of infants.

I. APHORISME.

BEcaufe the Anabaptiftes do oppugne the Baptifme of infants, as a point difagreeing with Chriftes inftitution : it is needfull to know the reafons,whereby the Baptifme of infants is proued by the fcriptures: and next to fhewe the vanitie and weakeneffe of the Anabaptiftes argumēts which they bring to the contrarie.

II.

Now then that the children of the faithfull ought to be baptifed may be fhewed out of Gods word by foure fpeciall arguments . The firft is from the example of Circūcifion , which affuredly had the like *a* reafon & the fame fignification that baptifme hath . For like as by Circumcifion

a Col.2.11. 12.

God

God teſtified to the people of Iſraell the
[b] remiſſion of ſinnes and [c] regeneration: ſo
by Baptiſme doth he promiſe the very
ſame things vnto the Chriſtians. If therefore their infants then, at Gods[d] cōmande-
ment were Circumciſed : it is a good conſequent that the children of the faithfull
vnder the Goſpell be baptiſed.

b Rom.4.1:
c Deut.30.6
Rom 2.29,
Coloſſ.2. 11
d Gen.17.12
Leuit.12. 3.

III.

For albeit we haue no ſuch charge for
the baptiſing of infants: yet we know right
well the Lordes good pleaſure herein by
the very nature and end of Baptiſme: eſpe-
cially ſeeing Baptiſme is ordained to ſucceede in the [a] place of Circumciſion. Now
the charge giue to them of old which profeſſed the Iewiſh Religion , was, that they
ſhould not onely be Circumciſed them
ſelues , but alſo all [b] the males that did belong vnto them . Wherefore in like manner ſuch as profeſſe Chriſtian Religion,
they are bounde to bring their infants to
be baptized.

a Col.2. 11.
12.

b Exo.12.48.

IIII.

Againe , the children of the faithfull
are partakers of that, which is ſignified by

Baptiſme, that is, the remiſſion of ſinnes, & regeneration, for they belong to Gods *Gene.17.7 'couenant wherein theſe benefits are pro- Act.2.39. 1.Cor.7.14.* miſed: with what colour then of reaſon ſhall we denie them the ſeale of the coue- nant?

V.

And if our infants may not be baptized, then the grace of God by Chriſts cōming doth leſſe appeare vnto vs then vnto the Iewes in times paſt: for that the faithfull Iewes were confirmed by the ſeale of Cir- cumciſion cōcerning the ſaluatiō of their children: wherefore it is againſt all reaſon that Chriſtiās ſhould not in like maner by the teſtimonie of Baptiſme be aſſured of the ſaluation of their infants.

VI.

Laſtly the children of the faithfull ought *Mat.19.14* to be offred 'vnto Chriſt, as they that haue communion with him in the kingdome of heauen: therfore we muſt giue them their Baptiſme, as the ſeale of that communiō, and heritage, they haue with Chriſt in heauen.

For

VII.

For whereas the Anabaptiftes denie
that the baptizing of infantes was vfed in
the Apoftles time : we muft know that
the old writers fay contrarie: and the fame
may alfo appeare by the Acts of the Apo-
ftles(which Luke a companion of the A-
ftles, as eye-witneffe of all the things, for
the moft part, hath left written for the
Church of Chrift) where it *is fayd in* *a* Act.2.38.
the wordes of Peter to the Iewes con- 39.
uerted by his Sermon, that they be baptized for the remiffion of fins, and that they
fhould receiue the gift of the holy Ghoft,
for that this promife was made not onely
vnto them, but vnto their childrẽ. VVhere
in the word (children) it can not be de-
nied,but that infants muft be vnderftood.
Againe , this Euangelift recordeth that
Paule & Silas(in whofe companie he him
felf alfo was)baptized *Lydia & her houfe*, *b* Act.16.15.
and the Iayler *with all his houfhold.* *c* Ibid v.33.

VIII.

Next,whereas they fay that infants may
not be baptized, becaufe they can not cõ-
ceiue the doctrine of faith & repentance:

L iij

The like reafon might be made againft the Circumcifion of infants. Wherefore it fufficeth that they are baptized vnto the repentance and faith to come, euen as the infants among the Iewes were Circumcifed.

IX.

Thirdly, whereas they obiect that Baptifme was giuen for the remiffion of fins: and that infants haue not finned : the affumption is falfe : for albeit infants haue not finned, after the like manner of the transgreffion of [a] Adam, that is actually in their own perfon : yet they finned in [b] him or in his loynes : for that they are [c] dead in him, and [d] dye dayly no leffe then fuch as be of yeares.

[a] Rom.5.14.
[b] Ibid.v.12.
[c] 1.Cor.15.22.
[d] Rom.5.14. and 6.21.

X.

Fourthly, whereas they fay that Chrift hath cleanfed [a] his Church *by the washing of water*, and that infantes haue no neede of this cleanfing, becaufe they be not vncleane : againe, the affumption is falfe : for [b] Dauid confeffeth that he was conceiued in finne: and for that the infants of the faithfull are members of the Church : it followeth

[a] Ephe.5.26.
[b] Pfal.51.7.
[c] 1.Cor.7.14

followeth that they alſo are purged by the
bloud of Chriſt : and therefore we muſt
graunt them the ſeale thereof which is
Baptiſme.

XI.

Laſtly, where they ſay, that none in the
Apoſtles time was baptized, but he that
made profeſſion of his faith before: that is
true onely of ſuch as were ² of yeares : but
that the infants of ſuch as profeſſed the
faith, and were baptized, were alſo baptized in like manner, we haue before plainly proued in the 7. Aphoriſme.

a Act.2.41.
Act 8.12.
Ibid.v.37.38.

CHAP. XXVI.

Of the Lordes Supper.

I. Aphorisme.

THe Supper of the Lord, is the ſecond
Sacrament of the ² new Teſtament or
couenant of grace, wherein by the ᵇ breaking of bread and powring of the wine into the cup, the paſſion & ſhedding of the
bloud of Chriſt, is figured, repreſented,
& as it were ſet before our eyes, and next
by giuing, taking, eating and drinking of

a Mat 26.28
Mar.14.24.
Luke.22.20.
1.Cor.11.25
b Mat 26.26
Mar.14 22.
Luke.22.19.
1.Cor.11.24

c Mat.26.28
d Iohn.6. 51.
53.54.58.
these elementes,the 'promiſe of the ʳremiſſion of ſinnes,and life euerlaſting(purchaſed by the paſſion of Chriſt,and by his bloud ſhed,& in a word, by that his precious death)& the promiſe of their cōmu-

e 1.Cor.10.
16.17.and c.
12.verſ 13.
nion 'as members with their head Chriſt Ieſus,is ſealed to all the beleeuing & worthy receiuers; wherby it cōmeth to paſſe, that the faithful ſweetly reſt in the fauor of God.obtained for them by his ſons death:

f 1.Cor.3.7 8
and ſo feed with him ſpiritually,and dayly grow vp in a holy communiō with Chriſt.

II.

And that the holy Supper is a Sacramēt of the new couenant, it may appeare by the very words of the inſtitution,which the Lord pronounced of the cup ſaying, *This cup is the new Teſtament or couenant in my bloud*, that is, a Sacrament of the new couenant.

III.

We call the Lordes Supper,the ſecond Sacrament of the new Teſtament, in reſpect of Baptiſme which is the firſt. For like as in the old Teſtament, there were two principall Sacramēts, Circumciſiō & **the**

the Paſſeouer, ſo there are two in the new,
Baptiſme, and the Lordes Supper, which
directly anſwer them & ſucceede in their
places. And as none was admitted to the
Paſſeouer, but the ᵃ Circumciſed : ſo none ᵃ Exo. 12.48
muſt be receiued to the Supper, but the
Baptized.

IIII.

The commandement of Chriſt contained in the inſtitution, is in theſe wordes:
Take ye, and eate ye : Take ye, and drinke ye,
and do this in remembrance of me.

V.

Againe, it is manifeſt by the wordes of
the inſtitution, that Chriſt vſed bread and
wine in this Sacrament.

VI.

In the breaking of bread in the Lordes
Supper, we follow both the Lordes ᵃ cō- ᵃ Mat.26. 26.
maundement, and his ᵇ example : for the Mar.14.22.
                                          Luke. 22. 19.
Lord did not onely breake the bread, and 1.Cor.11.24.
ſo by breaking it, did conſecrate the ſame ᵇ Ibid.
a Sacrament of his body, but alſo commãded this bread ſo bleſſed & ſo broken, to
be receiued, and eaten, as the liuely ſymbole and Sacrament of his precious body

broken, that is, crucified for vs . And the
c 1.Cor. 11. 23.
ᶜ Apostle faith, that he receiued of the
Lord which he deliuered to the Corinthians concerning the adminiſtration of this
d 1.Cor. 10.16
Sacrament: and this ᵈbreaking of bread
he both commaunded & commended vnto them. To be ſhort then, the breaking
of bread, is an eſſentiall ceremonie in the
Lordes Supper: for that this is the principall end thereof to repreſent, feale and fet
e 1.Cor. 11. 24.
before vs the paſſion and breaking of ᵉthe
body of Chriſt. The fame reaſon is of the
powring forth of the wine, if we cōpare it
with the ſhedding of the bloud of Chriſt.

VII.

The paſſion of Chriſt is fet before vs in
this Sacrament in a liuely manner, as by
a Gal 3.1.
ᵃpreaching of the Goſpell.

VIII.

We receiue Ieſus Chriſt and his holy
ſpirite moſt comfortably by the word: for
it is Gods holy ordinance and inſtrument
to cōuay his graces into our minds, harts,
and conſcie3ces, and that mighty power
to confer and giue vs the ſpirite of grace,
the ſpirite of faith, the ſpirite of adoption,
the

the fpirit of fanctificatiõ, of wifedome.&c.

IX.

But there is difference betweene the participation of Chriſt by the one and by the other, for the Lord firſt by his word confers grace, but grace and faith once giuen, are ſtrengthned and increaſe day-ly by the Sacraments.

X.

Againe, the Lord by the word, workes onely by one fenfe in vs, namely the fenfe of hearing, whereby comes knowledge & fo faith. Rom. 10.14.15. And this fenfe in deede is now fince the corruption of our nature, the fenfe of learning and vnder-ſtanding, and fo the principall to breed & beget faith in vs : but before the fall of A-dam the fight (I take it) was the principall fenfe to receiue and learne wifedome and vnderſtanding in the vewe and confidera-tiõ of the workes of God. The Lord ther-fore in the Sacrament, hath refpect to the fight and all other fenfes: for in and by the Sacrament the foule doth not onely heare Chriſt (as in the word) but alfo fee Chriſt, touch Chriſt, fmell & taſt, and fo feed vpõ

See Brad-fords Sermõ of the Sup-per.

Chrift and all his benefites.

XI.

The principall parts of this Sacrament are, to feale and ratifie that promife of Chrift,wherin he affureth vs that his flefh

a Iohn 6. 55. is a meate indeed, and his bloud is drinke indeede, to feed vs vnto life euerlafting:

b Ibid.v.51. and in that he faith he is the b bread of life, whereof who fo eateth fhall liue for euer: it is ordained (I fay) to feale that promife, and to this effect to fend vs vnto the croffe of Chrift , where that promife was per-formed and fulfilled in euery refpect. For the flefh of Chrift was made vnto vs the bread of life, or that meate which quicke-

c Ibid. neth vs,in that it was c crucified for vs.

XII.

This meate we can not eate , but by

a Iohn 6.35. a faith, and this drinke we can not b drinke
b Ibidem. but by faith.

XIII.

Againe, to eate the flefh of Chrift by faith , and to drinke his bloud by faith , is to receiue by faith the promife of God, which teftifieth that the flefh of Chrift, was crucified for vs, & that his bloud was

fhed

shed for vs, that is, for the remiſſion of our ſinnes.

XIIII.

The fruite which followeth this ſpirituall meate and drinke, is a ſpirituall [a] ioy in God, and the increaſe of our [b] communion with Chriſt: for this dependeth vpon the confirmation of our faith.

a Iohn.6.57.
1.Cor.5.8.
b 1.Cor.10.
17.

XV.

Againe, it is very manifeſt that the body of Chriſt, is not eaté with the [1] mouth, and that his body is not contained [2] in the bread of the holy Supper, for that [a] heauē muſt containe him vnto the day of iudgement. Neither may we ſay that the body of Chriſt is euery where, that it may be in heauen at one and the ſelfe ſame time, & here on earth alſo in the bread of the Lordes Supper, for it euer retaines that propertie of a mans body, which is to be finite, for *Chriſt was made like vnto vs in all* [b] *things,* [c] *ſinne onely excepted.*

1.Tranſubſtantiation.
2.Conſubſtantiation.
a Aἑ.3.21.

b Heb.2.17.
c Heb.4.15.

XVI.

Againe, if the body of Chriſt, and the bloud of Chriſt, were cōtained vnder the formes of bread and wine: the one part

muſt be neceſſarily ſeuered from the o-
ther,and ſo Chriſt muſt dye againe : But
Chriſt dyeth ᵃno more.

a Rom.6.9.

XVII.

Now that the bread of the Lords Supper,is not tranſubſtantiated into the body
of Chriſt ,but that the ſubſtaunce of the
bread remaineth after the wordes of con-
ſecration,it may appeare , for that Chriſt
would teach by this bread ,as by a verie
apt ſimilitude ,that his fleſh is ᵃſpirituall
meate: therefore it muſt neceſſarily be very bread,that we may aſſuredly conclude,
that our ſoules are as truly fed with Chriſt
crucified for vs, as our bodies are truly fed
with that bread,which there is broken for
vs,and giuen vs.Againe, Chriſt commanded all the faithfull to eate of one ᵇbread:
to teach that they all,ᶜare , as one bread,
or as one body : therefore it muſt be very
bread ,that the ſimilitude may continue,
that like as of many grains or maſſe one
ſubſtance is made, & ſo one bread ,ſo the
faithfull being many ,hauing one ſpirit of
faith to knit them vnto Chriſt,and one
ſpirite of loue to knit them,one with another,

a Iohn.6.55.

b 1.Cor.10.
17.
c Ibidem.

ther, are made one Church , as one body
in and through their head Iefus Chrift.

XVIII.

And like as neither the water of Baptifme is chaunged , nor that water which
ftreamed from the ᵃ rocke being fmitten
with Mofes rod , was chaunged into the
bloud of Chrift: and yet both Sacraments
of the fame : So in like maner, the wine in
the Lords Supper is not changed into the
bloud of Chrift , wherof notwithftanding
it is a Sacrament , as Chrift ordained and
appointed.

ᵃ Num. 20.
10. 11.

XIX.

And yet we do not goe from the verie
words of Chrift , but defire to giue them
their naturall fenfe and meaning.

XX.

The verie naturall fenfe of the words of
Chrift , doth depend vpon a Metonymie,
or trope , whereby the name of the thing
fignified , that is the bodie , is attributed
to the figne which is bread: and fo for the
cup and bloud of Chrift in like maner.

XXI.

This Metonymicall or Sacramentall

phrafe is vfed euerie where in Scripture, where the holy Spirit fpeaketh of Sacraments. For we may not otherwife vnderftand thefe places; as where it is fayd, that circumcifion is the [a] couenant of God, & the pafchall lambe is [b] the Lords Paffeouer in Ægypt, and the [c] facrifices of the Law are fayd to expiate the finnes of the people, and that the rocke which gaue thē water to drinke in the wildernefle was [d] Chrift.

a Gen.17.10
b Exod.12.
11.and 27.
c Leuit.6.30.
&c.

d 1.Cor.10.4

XXII.

The holy Spirit vfually retaineth this maner of fpeaking in all Sacraments for two caufes principally: firft to helpe vs againft our ignorance, dulnefle, and the blindnefle of our hearts: for if the Lord fpake not on this maner, we would but only faften our eyes and our hearts vpon the bare fignes and ceremonies, and content our felues (as haue hypocrites in all ages) with bare and emptie fhadowes, without faith, feare, repentance, obedience, or any reuerence of the holy couenant. Therfore I fay, the Lord firft fpeakes on this wife, to lift vp our hearts and foules by faith to
behold,

Pfal 50.

behold, confider , and to feede vpon the
things fignified. The fecond caufe of the
vfe of this phrafe in the Sacraments is,for
that the verie truth is fo , there is a reall
prefence of the figne and the thing fignified to the beleeuer, for as he doth bodily
and really participate of the figne, fo doth
he fpiritually,& as really receiue and feed
vpon the thing fignified.

Sacramenta
funt figna
exhibentia
non fignifi-
cantia tantû.

XXIII.

And thus fpeaketh Auguftine alfo,left
any thinke of this,as of fome new inuêtiô.
If Sacraments had not a certaine fimilitude
of thofe things , of which they be Sacramêts,
furely they should be no Sacraments: and by
reafon of this likeneffe , they haue often the
names of the things,(which are fignified by
them.)*Therfore as the Sacrament of the bo-*
dy of Chrift , is after a certaine manner , the
body of Chrift;the Sacrament of the bloud of
Chrift, the bloud of Chrift : fo the Sacrament
of faith is faith.

a Epift.23.ad
Bonifac.

Whereas they obiect that it is not like
that when Chrift would minifter vnto his
Apoftles,a fpeciall comfort in aduerfitie,
that then he fhould fpeake darkely and

M

doubtfully: the matter it felf fheweth that
this metonymicall phrafe feemed not
hard or obfcure vnto the Apoftles : for if
they had not thought that the Lord called
the bread his body, becaufe it is a liuely &
true figne & Sacrament thereof, out of all
queftion they had bene much troubled &
difquieted with fo prodigious a matter,
which neceffarily followeth from the lite-
rall fenfe of the word : & this may yet better appeare, for the fame verie time they
could not well conceiue and vnderftand

a Ioh.14.5.8   more eafie and common *a* argumentes.
&c.16.v.17.   Therefore (I fay) for that they were not
troubled with thefe wordes, it is manifeft
that they vnderftood them metonymically, after the maner of the Scripture:& the
rather for that a little before, they had eaten of the lambe, which in the fame fenfe
was called the paffeouer : for that it was a
fymbole of that memorable paffeouer,

b Exo.12.27.   wherein the Angell *b* of the Lord fmiting
all the firft borne of the Ægyptians, did
paffe ouer the houfes of the people of Ifraell: by which occafiõ they were brought
out of Ægypt, and fo freed from that ex-
treme

treme bondage.

XXV.

They fpend here wind in vaine to obiect the omnipotencie of God, to fhewe
that the bodie of Chrift, may be both in
heauen and in the Sacramentall bread at
one and the fame time. For the queftion
is not here, what God can do, but what he
will do, and what his will and good pleafure is. And his will is, that Chrift be like
his brethren in *all things finne onely* [b] excepted. Therefore his will is, that he haue
a true bodie, that is, a finite bodie, and li-
mited in place. Againe, albeit God be
omnipotent, yet can he not effect contraries, as that any thing at one time both be,
and be not, for that he can not [c] lye nor denie [d] himfelfe, for this is againft his nature. And thefe propofitions or fentences
are meere contradictorie; Chriftes bodie
is a true bodie: Chriftes body is not a true
bodie, but an infinite.

a Heb.2.17.
b Heb.4.15.

c Tit.1.2.
Heb.6.18.
d 2.Tim.2 13

XXVI.

Neither yet fhall this helpe the aduer-
faries, to fay, that vnleffe it be graunted,
Chriftes bodie is euery where, it will ne-

ceſſarily follow, that it is ſeuered from the diuine nature, which is euery where, and whereunto it is perſonally vnited : for although Chriſts body be not euery where, but contained in one certaine place, yet neuertheleſſe it is euer perſonally vnited to the Deitie of the *word* for the perſonall vnion doth not make equall the humane nature with the diuine, or change the properties of the diuine nature into the humane : that the humane nature may haue the ſame proprieties with the diuine : but is ſuch an vniō as that therby the humane nature ſubſiſteth in the perſon of the *word* ; ſo that it is as a part thereof, neither hath it by it ſelfe, or without the *word* any ſubſiſting. Therefore well ſpake the fathers in the Councell of Chalcedon. *The difference of natures in Chriſt, is not taken away becauſe of the vnion* (of them:) *but rather* (by this doctrine of the vnion of natures) we learne, *that the proprieties of both natures are kept, as concurring and meeting together into one perſon or* * *ſubſtance.*

Chriſt is that word. Iohn.1.1.

* *Hypoſtaſis.*

Seeing

XXVII.

Seeing therefore the bodie of Chriſt is finite and taken vp from earth to ᵃ heauen, and muſt be contained there vntill the ᵇ day of iudgement, it followeth that it is not in all places, nor in the Sacramentall bread included.

ᵃ Act.19.10. 11.

ᵇ Act.3 21. 1.Cor.11.26

XXVII.

And albeit we ſay that Chriſtes body is in heauen, and no where elſe, according to the true proprietie of a body: yet we tye it not to any certaine place in heauen: but we iudge him to be there free, as it beſeemeth and is conuenient for that celeſtiall glory: which to ſearch into, we deeme alſo to be a vaine and bold curioſitie.

XXIX.

Whereby it is very manifeſt that they ſlaunder vs, which ſay that we tye the body of Chriſt to a certaine place in heauen.

XXX.

And whereas yet they ſay, that albeit Chriſts body be in heauen viſible, yet this letteth not, but that it may be in the Sacramentall bread in an inuiſible manner: firſt they can not proue this by the Scrip-

M iij

tures , next they ſpeake flat contradicto-
ries againſt themſelues ; when as they ſay
that Chriſt is in the bread really , ſubſtantially, corporally; if that be ſo , he muſt be
there alſo in a viſible manner. For whatſoeuer humane bodie is any where ſub-
ſtātially, the ſame is there alſo viſibly. For
this *viſibilitie* is a propertie, which cā not
be ſeuered from the ſubſtaunce of mans
bodie. For this cauſe Chriſt when he appeared after his reſurrection to his Apoſtles, & deſired to ª proue that his very body was there preſent ſubſtantially, he rea-
ſoneth(if ſo I may ſpeake)frō the * viſibilitie and * palpabilitie thereof; and ſo ap-
pealeth to the very ſenſes of his Diſciples,
that they might teſtifie the truth of his reſurrection.

a Luk.24.36.
37.3 8.39.

*That which
may be ſeen.
*That which
may be tou-
ched & felt.

XXXI.

And whereas yet they make an other
exception, that it is vnmeet to ſubmit the
nature of a glorious body, to the lawes of
common nature: that makes nothing to
proue the inuiſible preſence of Chriſtes
bodie in the Sacramentall bread. For the
glorie ª hath not aboliſhed the truth of the
body,

a Luk. 23 36
&c.
Act 7 55. 56.
& 1.9.10. 11.

bodie, wherein the vifibilitie thereof is
contained. Next this alfo is to be confidered, that in that firſt Supper of Chriſt
with his Difciples, that his body was not
yet glorified: and there is none other celebration of the Lordes Supper now, then
was at that time.

XXXII.

And albeit we deny the body of Chriſt
to be included in the Sacramentall bread:
yet we fay not that Chriſt is altogether &
in euery refpect abfent from his holy Sa-
crament:or that the bread & wine be but
bare and emptie fignes. For Chriſt is truly prefent by the grace of his holy fpirite,
where two or three ᵃ are gathered toge-　*ᵃ Mat.18.20.*
the in his name:and lifteth vp alfo euen to
heauen vnto himfelfe the hearts of the
faithfull by the promife of the Gofpell:
that they may contemplate there(name-
ly in the heauenly ᵇ fanctuarie)that his fa-　*ᵇ Heb.9.11.*
crifice, which he offred for them vpon his　²⁴·
Croffe, and by faith feed thereupon vnto
life euerlaſting.

XXXIII.

Againe, if the body of Chriſt be not in
M iiij

the Sacramentall bread, it followeth alſo
that we muſt not adore his body there: but
we muſt worſhip and adore him in heauē,

◄ Col.3.1. where he ſitteth at the right hand of God
the father: whither alſo in elder ages, in
the celebration of the Lordes Supper, the
people were inuited, when they were put
in minde of the place, with *ſurſum corda,*
lift vp your harts vnto the Lord.

XXXIIII.

Neither muſt the Lordes Supper be a
diuine action, performed by the Miniſter
of the Church alone, but the Paſtor muſt
declare and lay open with a good voyce,
and in a plaine manner, what the miſterie
thereof is, vnto the people.

XXXV.

In like manner we muſt reiect priuate
communions, as when this Sacrament is
adminiſtred to particular perſons readie
to dye, without any congregation or
companie of the faithfull to be partakers
with him of that holie communion: for
the Apoſtle ſpeaking of the celebration

◄ 1.Cor 11. of the Supper, ſaith, *when ye meet toge-*
20. *ther:* againe, for that this Sacrament is
a ſpe-

a fpeciall fymbole, of the communion of Saintes : and this the Apoftle meaneth where he faith, *for* [b] *we that are many are one bread, and one body, becaufe we all are partakers of one bread.*

[b] 1.Cor. 10. 17.

XXXVI.

The worthineffe of the communicants confifteth in this that they [a] acknowledge and bewayle their owne vnworthineffe, and by faith call vpon God, that he will of his grace and mercy in Iefus Chrift make them worthy.

[a] 1.Cor.11. 28.

XXXVII.

Yet to fpeake more diftinctly & plainly to the vnderftanding of the ignorant, to the end they may come prepared and aduifedly to the holy Communion, and for that the abufe of this holy Sacrament, is one caufe of all thefe iudgements which are paft and haue confumed many, and yet are ftill threatned againft vs: therefore the vnworthy receiuers which difhonour God, hurt and hinder their owne faluation, and prouoke Gods wrath againft his Church and people, they are thefe which follow.

XXXVIII.

1   In the firſt place I ſet all Atheiſts, mē

a Ephe.2.12   *without God, without ¹Chriſt*, or any Reli-
Pſal.14.1.   gion, meere Epicures in the world, therefore ought they to be without this holy
Sacrament: they be vnworthy of this holy
communion, for they be not in communion with God and his people.

2   All vncleane beaſts, doggs, & ſwine,
I meane all in the Church of an vncleane
beaſtly life: ſuch as the Apoſtle aſſureth
vs cā not enter into the kingdome of hea-
1.Cor.6.9.   uen: *fornicators, idolaters, adulterers, wan-*
tōs, buggerers, theeues, couetous, drunckards,
raylers, extortioners; a watch-word is added, *be not deceiued*. Theſe be vnworthy
our priuate feaſtes, how much more to
meet with vs, our Lord and Sauiour Ieſus
Chriſt in this holy banquet.

Ignorant in   3   All ignorant people (howſoeuer they
the great   may ſeeme harmeleſſe, &c.) which cā not
grounds of   *diſcerne the Lordes body*. 1. Cor. 11. v. 29.
Religion.   nor yet deſire to diſcerne and know it: No
Heb. 6.1.2.3.   knowledge, no faith: no faith, no loue: no
4 5.   loue, no affiance or truſt in God: no truſt,
no feare: no feare, no humiliation: want
theſe

thefe graces, or any of them, no worfhip, no acceffe to God. Heb.11.6. Therefore thefe be vnworthy receiuers.

4 Such as lightly account of the coue-nant, whatfoeuer loue and zeale they pre-tend to the Sacramentes: Such as defpife the one, are and muft be prophane con-temners of the other. Pfal.50.16.

5 Some foolifh wits pretend loue and great zeale to the word, and yet neglect and contemne the holy Sacraments: their contempt appeareth in the breach of the Lordes ordinance, they feldome come to the Lordes Supper (as they are bound) to preach and celebrate with vs the bleffed comemoration of the Lordes death vntill his comming againe. 1.Cor.11.24.25.26.

6 All fuch as do not hunger for Chrift, for they can not feed on Chrift: no know-ledge of finne, no feeling of finne : no fee-ling of finne, no forow for finne: no forow for finne, no confeffion of finne : no con-feffion of finne, no defire of grace : no de-fire of grace, no fpirite of faith to receiue Chrift: no fpirite of faith, no fpirite of a-doption, fanctification, &c.

Pfal.32.5.
Ephe.1.15.
Rom.8.14.15

7 All contentious brethren, for this is a Sacrament of our vnitie, badge of loue, and a band of vnion and communion with Chriſt & all his holy members. 1. Cor. 10. 2.16.

Iohn. 1. 12. 8 All vnbeleeuers, for all ſuch as want the precious faith, haue no hand to receiue Chriſt: they receiue onely as Auguſtin ſpeaketh, and as Iudas did *panem Dominū, the bread of the Lord, not, panem Domini, the bread of life, the Lord Chriſt.*

9 The faithfull alſo in regard of their frailtie, weakneſſe, corruptions, and manifold wants, if they haue not duly, truly, and wiſely, examined, humbled, and ſo prepared thēſelues to meet Ieſus Chriſt, they be vnworthy: and ſo they cauſe many plagues, many afflictions and euils in this life, vpō their bodies & ſoules, that being iudged & chaſtened here, they may eſcape the condēnation of the world in the life to come. 1. Cor. 11. 28. 30. 31. And thus farre of vnworthy receiuers.

XXXIX.

That forme of adminiſtration of the Lords Supper is beſt, which cometh nea-
reſt

reſt the ſimplicitie of the firſt inſtitution,
& is furtheſt from ſuperſtition:wherin albeit,there be ſome things indifferent , yet
the breaking of bread for the ᵃcauſes be-   ᵃ Aphoriſ.6.
fore alledged , may not be counted an indifferent thing.

XL.

And albeit the Lord hath not appointed any certaine times for the celebration
of the Lordes Supper:yet reaſon ſo requireth that Chriſtians haue it in often vſe,
that they may ofte remember the paſſion
of Chriſt:& by this commemoration confirme their faith and ſtir vp themſelues to
prayſe & magnifie the goodnes of God in
the worke of their redemptiõ: & finally to
increaſe the mutuall loue,& to teſtifie the
ſame one to another, cõſidering the band
thereof in the vnitie of the bodie of our
Lord and Sauiour Ieſus Chriſt.

CHAP. XXVII.

Of the Popish Maſſe.

I. Aphorisme.

THe Papiſts faine that the Maſſe is a
worke , wherein the Maſſe-prieſt
doth create or make his Chriſt of

bread, by buzzing or mumbling of these fiue words, *Hoc est enim corpus meum : for this is my bodie.* And then offereth him to the Father as a sacrifice, to expiate the sins of all, quicke, and dead, for whom that Masse is celebrated.

II.

This opinion of prophane Papistes, is impious and blasphemous. For first this reproch and disgrace is offered thereby vnto Christ : that he is not the only Priest of the new Testament.

a Heb. 5.6.
and 7.24.

III.

Againe, this doctrine ouerthroweth the merite of Christs death : as if the sins of all the faithfull were not perfectly expiate by that one ᵃ sacrifice of Christes death.

a Heb. 9.12.
and 10.12.14.

IIII.

Thirdly, the Papistes by this assertion, as much as lyeth in them, do againe crucifie Christ : in that they promise the remission of sinnes by the Masse, and so set vp a new Testament : and in that they say they offer vp Christ as an host or sacrifice vnto God. For where there is a Testamēt,

there

there muft needs be the ª death of a tefta-   *ª* Heb.9.16.
tor : & where an hoft is, it muft be flaine.

V.

Fourthly, this opinion or affertion doth
depriue vs of the benefit of Chrifts death,
that is, the remiffion of finnes: for if finnes
be pardoned by the merite of the Maffe,
then furely are they not pardoned by the
merite of the ª death of Chrift.   *ª* Mat.26.28.

V I.

Fiftly, the Maffe doth vtterly euert and
take away the Lords Supper: for it cannot
ftand with it. For in the Supper the Lords
purpofe is to giue a bleffing ª vnto vs : but *ª* Ioh.6.32.
in the Maffe men purpofe to offer vp fatif-
faction vnto God. Againe, in the Supper
the Lord teftifieth vnto vs, that we are &
muft be daily ᵇ quickened, by the onely fa- *ᵇ* Ioh.6.57.
crifice of Chrift : but in the Maffe they
faine, that Chrifts facrifice cannot profite
vs, if it be not iterated euerie day. Thirdly,
the Supper is celebrated by the ᶜ whole *ᶜ* 1.Cor.11.
congregation, but the Maffe is celebrated 18.& 10.17.
by the Prieft onely.   Mat.26.27.

V I I.

Moreouer, the arguments which Papiſts vſe for the defence of the Maſſe, are of no waight, as theſe following: Chriſt ſayd in the inſtitution of the Supper, *Do this*: therefore he commaunded his Apoſtles and their ſucceſſours to offer vp or ſacrifice his bodie vnto God. For ſo this word *facere, to do it*, (ſay they) is vſed euerie where in holy [a] Scripture, and ſo it is found alſo with [b] prophane writers. But I ſay it is no good conſequent, that becauſe that word is elſewhere ſo taken, that therfore it is alſo ſo vſed in this place. Next, that it muſt haue here another ſignificatiõ, it is euident, both by the coherence oſentéces, & by the Apoſtle [c] Paules expoſition, that nothing elſe is ſignified, but this, *Eate this bread, and drinke ye of this cup*. Againe thoſe words were not ſpoken to the Apoſtles onely, as Miniſters of the Church (for Chriſt himſelfe performed the partes of a Miniſter) but as to all the faithfull receiuing the Sacrament at the hands of the Lords Miniſter. Wherefore theſe wordes doe no leſſe concerne thoſe whom they call lay men, then they do the Prieſts or Miniſters of the Church.

Againe,

[a] Exod 29. Num.28.
[b] Apud Vergil.eclog.3.
[c] 1.Cor.11. 26.

VIII.

Againe, if the Supper be to repreſent Chriſtes ſacrifice and oblation, which he made vpon his Croſſe: thē Chriſt muſt be offered vp in the Sacramēt of the Supper, for how can we otherwiſe repreſent in the Supper the oblation of Chriſt, but by offering vp Chriſt vnder the kindes of bread and wine. But this conſequence is falſe, and ſo is the reaſon thereof. For that oblation which Chriſt made on the Croſſe, both may & muſt be otherwiſe repreſented, that is, by the [a] breaking of the bread and the powring out of the wine.

[a] 1.Cor.11. 24.

IX.

Againe, if the paſcall lambe was to be ſacrificed then Chriſt alſo in the Euchariſt muſt be ſacrificed, for that the paſchal lambe was a type of the Lordes Supper: here I anſwere againe, the conſequence is falſe, and the reaſon therof: for of that antecedent this will follow that Chriſt alſo muſt be ſacrificed: for that the lambe was a type of [a] Chriſt, not in the Eucharist, but on the Croſſe: where as Iohn ſaith, that was finiſhed which the lambe prefigured.

[a] 1.Cor.5.7.

[b] Ioh.19.36.

N

X.

Againe, they bring a place of Malach.
chap. 1. v. 11. *from the riſing of the ſunne,
vnto the going downe of the ſame, my name
is great among the Gentils, and in euery place
incenſe ſhalbe offred vnto my name and a
pure offring.* But I anſwer, that where they
inferre that the body of Chriſt is offred vp
in the Supper, becauſe it is a cleane or
pure offring, the argumēt is falſe, becauſe
it will not follow from the generall to the
ſpeciall affirmatiuely. And it is very manifeſt to any man of vnderſtanding, that Ma-
lachie here ſpeaketh, as the *Prophets, of
the ſpirituall worſhip of the new Teſtament, vnder the ſhadowes of the ceremoniall worſhip vſed in the old.

a See Ioel.2.
28. & Act.2.
17.

But it is ſtraunge that theſe men dare
be bold to bring argumēts for the defence
of their Maſſe in ſacrifice out of the Epiſtle to the Hebrues: for that the principall
doctrine of that Epiſtle doth plainly euert
all this Popiſh inuētion of the Maſſe, out
of the 5. chap. v. 1. they haue this ſaying.
*Euerie Prieſt is ordained, that he may offer
ſacrifices for ſinnes.* Therefore there are alſo

a Heb 5.1.
καθίσαται.

so in the new Testament, Priests properly
so called, which offer vp ... crifices for sins.
For that the Apostle vseth a verbe of the
present tense, I answer, it is very manifest,
in all the Apostles doctrine and speach in
that place, that he speaketh of the Priestes
of the old Testament, and of the sacrifices
which were types of Christes sacrifice, the
only sacrifice expiatorie for sinne. And so
the Apostle speaking of Leuitical Priests,
in all the Epistle vseth verbes of the present tense, as chap. 7. 9. 11. The reason of
that phrase is, to set the matter whereof
he speaketh, more manifestly before the
eyes of men.

XII.

Next they borow out of the 7. chap. the
type of Melchi-zedek: & they reason thus;
If Christ did not sacrifice himselfe in the
Supper in an vnbloudy sacrifice vnder, the
kindes of bread and wine, then was he neuer made Priest after the order of Melchi-zedek: But he was made, &c. as the A-
postle witnesseth in that chap. The reason
of the consequence is, becaufe Melchi-zedek offred vp vnto God bread and wine, I

answer, the consequéce is false, for Christ is called a Priest after the order of Melchi-zedek, principally for this cause, as the Apostle sheweth, because he is a priest *a* Heb.7.3. for *euer, as Melchi-zedek there is noted and described, *without father, without mother, without kinred.* Againe, the reason of their consequéce is false, for that Melchi-zedek did not offer bread and wine vnto *b* Gen.14.18 God, but brought forth *b* bread and wine, for the refection of Abraham and his seruants, and that this is there signified we may well vnderstand both by the Hebrue word *Hotzi*, and by the circumstance of that action in that place.

XIII.

Lastly, they haue this sentence out of *a* Heb 9.23. the 9.chap.*It is necessarie that the* *a* * *simili-*
* Exempla- *tudes of heauenly things, should be purified*
ria. *with such things: but the heauenly things*
themselues (are purified) *with better* * *sacri-*
*Suciais. *themselues* (are purified) *with better* * *sacri-*
Hostes, as *fices then these* . Ergo, with oblations of
they speake. Masses: because he speaketh in the plurall number, hostes. Therfore he speaketh not of the bloudie sacrifice of Christ, which was but one. But I answer that the Apostle

ftle there ftill keepeth his plurall number, taking one number for another, becaufe he continueth in the comparifon of the legall facrifices. And of thefe chaunges, we haue many examples, as Ruth.1.v.10. and chapter.2.v.20. And that the Apoftle there fpeaketh of that one facrifice of Chrift, may appeare by the fcope of that whole chap. for that nothing elfe is there intended, but to compare the Priefthood of Chrift, with the Leuiticall Priefthood, and to fhew how far that excelleth this.

Enallage *n.* chaunge of number.

XIIII.

And albeit we vtterly deny that the holy Supper of the Lord (which the Papiftes haue transformed into the monfter of the Maffe) to be a facrifice expiatorie for fin: yet we do willingly confeffe and profeffe it to be the facrifice * Euchariticall of the new Teftament, for that it was inftituted by the Lord for this ende, by this folemne rite to ᵃ fhew & fet forth his death, that we might magnifie him as our onely redeemer to the glorious prayfe of his name.

* Sacrifice of prayfe & thankes-geuing.

ᵃ 1.Cor.11. 26.

N iij

CHAP. XXVIII.

Of the Ciuill Magiſtrate.

I. Aphorisme.

BEcauſe ſome think the ciuill Magiſtrat is to be baniſhed out of the Church of God: & others giue him too much power: it is verie needefull alſo , that we know by gods word, whether this order be allowed of God , and how far the ciuill Magiſtrats power reacheth.

II.

Both which points the better to know, we muſt ſpeake of three things in order: firſt of the Magiſtrat, next of the lawes, & laſtly of the people.

III.

Of the Magiſtrat we muſt conſider alſo three things, whether his place & calling be approued of God, what his office is, & what authoritie he hath.

IIII.

It is manifeſt by the Scriptures that God approueth Magiſtracie or ciuill gouernement: as Pſal.82.v.1. *God ſtandeth in*
the

the aſſemblie of Gods,he iudgeth amõg Gods.
v.6.I ſayd ye are Gods,and ye are all the chil-
dren of the moſt high. Deut.1.v. 17. Moſes
ſaith ,*the iudgement is Gods .* So 2.Chron.
19.v.6.Iehoſaphat ſaith to the Iudges, *ye*
execute not the iudgements of mã, but of the
Lord. Prou.8. v.15. Wiſedome that is the
ſonne of God ſpeaketh.*By me kings raigne*
and princes decree iuſtice. Dan.2. v.21. *God*
taketh away kingdomes,& ſetteth vp kings.
Rom.13.v.1.Paule ſaith . *He that reſiſteth*
power,reſiſteth the ordinance of God.

V.

The office of the Magiſtrat is to be the
[a] keeper of both the Tables of Gods law:&
therefore his principall care muſt be to ſet
vp and to defend the [b] pure worſhip and
ſeruice of God. Next, to do iudgement
[c] and iuſtice,that is ,to puniſh the euill, to
defend and reward the good.

[a] Deut.17. 18.19.

[b] Deut.15.5. 2.King 23. 2.Chron. 29. [c] Ierem.22 3 Pſal.82.3 4. Rom.13 3.4. Gene.9 .6.

VI.

Againe, if neede ſo require , the Magiſtrat is bounde to defend the ſubiect with
[a] armes, and thoſe dominions which are
committed to his charge.

[a] Deut.20. Luke.3.14. Mat.8.10. Act.10.4.

VII.

Notwithſtanding, when Magiſtrates puniſh either their ſubiects or their enemies: they ought to haue a ſpeciall care, that they giue no place to their owne affections, but reſpect onely the diſcharge of their dutie.

VIII.

The Magiſtrate may by good right require and demaund of his ſubiectes [a] tributes and cuſtomes: and he may vſe the ſame, not onely for the diſcharge of his publike ſeruices, but alſo for the [b] honour of his houſe, and for the preſeruation of his owne ſtate and dignitie.

a Ro.13 6.7.
b 1.Sam. 8.
11.&c.
Gen.44.22.
23.
Dan.2.41.

IX.

And thus farre of the Magiſtrate: now for the lawes, we muſt firſt obſerue, that God hath three kindes of lawes: the law morall, ceremoniall and iudiciall.

X.

The ſumme of the Morall law is comprized in the [a] Decalogue, conſiſting in the loue of God and the neighbour: and for that it is an euerlaſting rule of iuſtice,

a Exod.20.
Deut.5.

it

it muſt continue euer in force.

XI.

The Ceremoniall law was the [a] peda-   *a* Gal.3.24.
gogie of the Iewes vntill the coming of
Chriſt: and therefore Chriſt being come,
it is [b] abrogated.   *b* Col.2.16.
Epheſ.2.15.]

XII.

The Iudiciall law in as much as it was
properly applyed to the Iewes, bindeth
not the Chriſtian Magiſtrate : yet in ap-
pointing the [a] puniſhments of grieuous   *a* Leu.24.16.
ſinnes, it bindeth no leſſe the Chriſtian   Deut.13.5.
Magiſtrate at this day, then it bound the
Magiſtrates of the Iewes.

XIII.

And thus farre of the lawes. The third
part is of the ſubiectes. The dutie of ſubiectes towards their Magiſtrates, firſt is,
to eſteeme of them and [a] reuerence them   *a* Rom.13.7
as the miniſters and meſſengers or [b] vice-   *b* Rom.13.4.
gerents of God: next, with readineſſe of
minde, and in all obſeruance to [c] obey   *c* Ibid.v.1.
them. Laſtly, not to intermeddle with   and 5.
  1.Pet.2.13.
publique affaires, nor to [d] enterpriſe anie   14.
thing without their commiſſion.   *d* 1.Pet.4.15

XIIII.

They are bound alſo to obey them that vniuſtly[a] and tyrannically rule ouer them: ſo long as they commaund nothing that God hath forbidden, and forbid nothing that God hath commaunded: for in this caſe we muſt keepe that rule of S. Peter: *VVe muſt obey*[b] *God more then men*, and that rule of Chriſt,[c] *Giue vnto Cæſar thoſe things which are Cæſars, and vnto God thoſe things which are Gods.*

[a] 1.Pet.1.18
Ier.27.12.

[b] Act.4.19.
and 5.29.
[c] Mat.22.21.

A

A SVPPLEMENT
OR ADDITION, FOR
THE CLEERING AND
opening of the doctrine of the
Lords Supper.

HEREAS our Lord Iesus Chriſt the 6. of Iohn ſaith in expreſſe words, that *his flesh is* ˢ *meate indeed, & his bloud is drinke indeed.* And again, ᵇ *Vnleſſe ye eate the fleſh of the ſonne of man, and drinke his bloud, ye haue no life in you* : For the right vnderſtanding of theſe wordes and doctrine, which at the firſt ſight ſeemeth ſo ſtrange, and to the Capernaites (whom Chriſt then taught) moſt repugnant to all reaſon: and that the ſame may miniſter côfort vnto our ſoules, which is the right end and vſe of this celeſtiall veritie, two queſtions principally muſt be côſidered. The firſt is, *VVhat kind*

ᵃ Ioh.6.55.

ᵇ Ibid.v.53.

of

of meate the flesh of Chriſt is? The ſecond,
How or in what maner this meate is to be ea-
ten? The ſame queſtion may be made alſo
cōcerning the cup, as *VVhat kind of drinke*
the bloud of Chriſt is? and *in what maner*
muſt we drinke the ſame? Now then as concerning the firſt queſtion : If the fleſh of
Chriſt bee meate indeede (as is before
ſhewed) it muſt be either a corporall or
ſpirituall foode. Corporall foode is that
which nouriſheth him bodily that feedeth thereupon , and this (to ſpeake after
the vſuall maner and properly) is called
meate. Spirituall food, is that whereby the
ſoule or ſpirit of him which eateth is fed
and nouriſhed : and this is called meate
improperly , tropically , metaphorically,
becauſe it hath the likeneſſe of meat, properly ſo called. For like as by natural food
ſo properly called, the bodie is nouriſhed
and ſuſtained : ſo by that ſpirituall meate
the ſpirit and ſoule of man is cheriſhed, &
as nouriſhed. The ſame reaſon and deſcri-
ption may be giuen of the corporall and
ſpirituall drinke. And now it is certaine,
that neither the fleſh of Chriſt is a corporall

rall food, nor his bloud corporall drinke:
for that no bodily ſubſtance is fed & pre-
ſerued either by the fleſh or by the bloud
of Chriſt: For, to effect this, the fleſh of
Chriſt muſt bee eaten with the mouth,
chewed with the teeth, ſwallowed vp, di-
geſted, and ſo turned into that nouriſhing
* iuyce in the ſtomach, whereof bloud is   * Chilus.
ingendred, and ſo deriued or ſent into all
partes of the bodie, to be vnited thereunto, or altred and chaunged into the ſubſtance thereof, that the body may receiue
his growth and preſeruation therby. And
ſo in like maner, the bloud of Chriſt, if the
bodie were to be nouriſhed thereby, muſt
be drunke vp with the mouth, ſwallowed,
&c. But theſe things are againſt all reaſon, and horrible to be ſpoken. And this
was the verie cauſe, why the Capernaites
did ſo tremble at the ſpeech of Chriſt,
touching the eating of his fleſh, & tooke
it ſo in euil part, ſaying; *How can this man*   c Ioh.6.52.
giue vs his fleſh to eate? and againe, *This is*   d Ibid.v.60.
an hard ſaying, who can heare it? For they
vnderſtood Chriſt to ſpeake thoſe words
of a bodilie food, which were to be taken

with the mouth, for the nourishment of the body. Wherefore seeing that it is manifest by these absurde consequents, that the flesh of Christ is no meate for the body: it followeth, that it must be a spirituall foode, and his bloud spirituall drinke, whereby the spirite and soule of man is fed and preserued vnto life euerlasting, like as mans body is nourished and kept in this temporall & fraile life, by corporall meat and drinke. And this Christ himselfe seemeth to haue said in these wordes. *It is* * *the spirite that quickneth, the flesh profiteth nothing, the wordes that I speake vnto you are spirite and life.* And whereas the most of the best interpreters of these times expounde these wordes, of Christes Deitie, as if the same were vnderstood by the word *spirite*: so that Christes meaning (as they say) is, that the power of quickning doth proceede from the Deitie of Christ: so that his flesh hath power to quicken vs, as it is the flesh of the sonne of God crucified for vs. This exposition no doubt is found and good, yet I thinke this be the most simple and naturall sense,

* Ibid.v.63.

if

if by the word *spirit* we vnderſtãd the holy
Ghoſt, that the meaning ſhould be thus:
my fleſh which I ſaid muſt be eaten, to attaine eternall life, profiteth nothing to effect this, if ye eate the ſame corporally, as
you Capernaites vnderſtand me : but it is
the ſpirit which quickneth, that is, the holy Ghoſt quickneth the harts of the faithfull, and nouriſheth them vnto life euerlaſting, by working in them effectually to
beleeue in me, and ſo to eate my fleſh and
to drinke my bloud ſpiritually, that is, by
faith, whereby they are well aſſured that
my fleſh was crucified for them, and my
bloud ſhed for them for the remiſſion of
their ſinnes. *The wordes,* therefore (ſaith
he) *which I ſpeake vnto you,* of the neceſſitie of eating my fleſh to attaine eternall
life : theſe wordes I ſay *are ſpirite and life,*
that is, muſt be vnderſtood of the effectuall working of the holy Ghoſt in the harts
of the elect, to worke eternall life in them,
euen by faith.

Moreouer, for the better vnderſtanding of this point, in what ſenſe, the fleſh
of Chriſt is, and may truly be ſaid to be

our fpirituall foode:we muft expreffe alfo
in what manner it is made meate for vs.
And this Chrift taught vs in very plaine
wordes, in that Sermon, where he faith, *I*

f v.51.

am that living bread(that is, the quickning
bread, or that bread that giueth life)*which
came downe from heauen* : *If any man shall
eate of this bread, he shall liue for euer , and
the bread that I will giue ,is my flesh ,which
I will giue for the life of the world* . In thefe
laft wordes , *which I will giue for the life of
the world,* Chrift fheweth in what maner
his flefh fhould be foode for vs , and that
is , in that he will giue it vnto the death,
for our life , that is , to merite for vs life e-
uerlafting, offring it as Prieft himfelfe , a
holy facrifice to God his father. And that
this is the naturall fenfe of this relatiue

* Quam ego
dabo.

* *which* in this place : as if the Lord had
faid, *quatenus eam dabo*,in that, or for that
I fhall giue it , it is verie manifeft by the
matter it felfe , which is handled in that
place . For if we fhall not fo vnderftand
thofe wordes , as tending to declare the
former maner of that thing which is here
intreated: then that word muft note fome
diui-

diuifion of a generall into fpecials, as if
Chrift had two kindes of flefh, of which
the one he would giue for the life of the
world, the other he would not giue. But
this interpretation is manifeftly falfe, and
contrary to the articles of our faith wher-
on we ground the truth of Chriftes incarnation. Therefore that expofition of the
relatiue *which* in this place is verie true
and natural, and vfed to declare the forme
and manner of that thing, which is there
propofed or difputed vpon. And the very
fame interpretation is there of the words
of the Lord in the inftitution of his holy
Supper, where, of that bread broken, he
fpeaketh on this wife; *This is my bodie,*
which is giuen, or broken for you, that is, in
* afmuch as, or for that it is broken or gi- * Quatenus.
uen for you. For that holie bread, or as
Paule calleth it, that bread of the Lord, is
not fimplie the Sacrament of the Lordes
bodie: that is, doth not fimplie fignifie
and teftifie that the Lord hath a true bodie: but fignifieth and teftifieth, that the
Lords body is broken or giuen for vs, that
is, was offred on the Croffe with the fee-

O

ling of Gods wrath, to make satisfaction for our sinnes. And in like manner must we speake and thinke of the other wordes, which the Lord pronounced, of the holy cup or wine: saying, *This is that my bloud of the new Testament or couenant, which is shed for you and for manie, for the remission of sinnes*: that is, in asmuch as, or for that *it is shed, &c*. By the premisses, it is now manifest, that the flesh of Christ hath in it the nature of meate, not simplie but in a certaine respect: that is, in asmuch as, it was crucified for vs. Like as the body is said to be visible, in respect of the colours thereof.

Now concerning the second question in what maner, we eate the flesh of Christ, and drinke his bloud: I answer: Such as the meate and drinke is, such must be the maner of the eating and drinking thereof: but the flesh of Christ is spirituall meate, and his bloud is spirituall drinke, as is a-foreshewed. Therefore the flesh of Christ is eaten spiritually or in a spirituall manner, and his bloud is drunke also in the same manner. Now to eate the flesh of

Christ

Chriſt and to drinke his bloud ſpiritually, is to eate with the mouth of the ſpirite, that is, of the ſoule, to wit, by faith. Again, to eate the fleſh of Chriſt by faith, and to drinke his bloud, is nothing elſe but to be-leeue in Chriſt, or to beleeue that the fleſh of Chriſt is crucified for thee, and that his bloud is ſhed for thee, for the re-miſſion of thy ſinnes. This Chriſt himſelfe ſheweth in the ſame Sermon, where he propoundeth two propoſitions or ſen-tences ſignifying one thing : which are theſe : *he that beleeueth* ᵃ *in me hath eter-* ᵍ v. 47. *nall life*, and ᵇ *he that eateth my fleſh, and* ᵇ v. 54. *drinketh my bloud hath eternall life* . The matter alſo, and argument there handled requires this interpretation of the words of Chriſt : for if he meant by that phraſe of eating his fleſh one thing, and by that of faith another thing : then this conſe-quent would follow, we muſt haue not one, but two wayes to life euerlaſting : one by eating the fleſh of Chriſt, the other by faith . But the way to eternall life is but one, which is Chriſt alone receiued by faith, or faith in Chriſt our Sauiour, both

come to one effect. And yet the better to vnderstand this point, consider a little what the nature of faith is. And this is knowen by his next and proper obiect, which is the Gospell, or that testimonie which God hath giuen vs of his loue and grace for and through Iesus Christ, for faith resteth vpon the Gospell as the blessed and infallible testimonie of God. And the Gospell testifieth of Christ, that is, of his person and office, and of all his benefites towardes vs:that is to say,that Christ is the only begotten sonne of God,which for our sake and for our saluation came downe from heauen, and was made man of the virgine Marie :that he liued an holy life according to the law of God, and hath brought vnto vs from the bosome of his father the counsell of God concerning our saluation :who being righteous suffered for vs that are vnrighteous vnder *Pontius Pylate*, was crucified, dead, &c. And like as the Gospell testifieth these things vnto vs; so the Sacramentes also testifie the same, for they are seales of the Gospell, and as it were, a Gospell seene and a
Gospell

Gospell felt . He therefore that beleeueth these holy testimonies of God , in so doing , he spiritually feedeth vpon the bodie of Christ & spiritually drinketh the bloud of Christ . And thus doth Augustine, expounde this place of Christ . *Vnlesse* (saith he) *ye eate the flesh of the sonne of man, and drinke his bloud , ye haue no life in you. He seemeth to commande a horrible fact , and a thing most detestable : It is a figure commanding vs to communicate with , or to become partakers of the Lordes passion, and to lay vp sweetely and comfortably in memorie , that his flesh was crucified and wounded for vs:* thus saith Augustine . After the same maner doth M[r] Iohn Caluin,that famous diuine of our age , lay open those wordes of Christ, in his booke of Institutions the 4. booke Chap.17.sect.5.

De doctri Christ. Lib cap.16.

FINIS.

O iij